Developing an Air Force Retention Early Warning System

Concept and Initial Prototype

DAVID SCHULKER, LISA M. HARRINGTON, MATTHEW WALSH,
SANDRA KAY EVANS, IRINEO CABREROS, DANA UDWIN,
ANTHONY LAWRENCE, CHRISTOPHER E. MAERZLUFT,
CLAUDE MESSAN SETODJI

Prepared for the Department of the Air Force
Approved for public release; distribution unlimited

 PROJECT AIR FORCE

T0321468

For more information on this publication, visit **www.rand.org/t/RRA545-1**.

About RAND

The RAND Corporation is a research organization that develops solutions to public policy challenges to help make communities throughout the world safer and more secure, healthier and more prosperous. RAND is nonprofit, nonpartisan, and committed to the public interest. To learn more about RAND, visit www.rand.org.

Research Integrity

Our mission to help improve policy and decisionmaking through research and analysis is enabled through our core values of quality and objectivity and our unwavering commitment to the highest level of integrity and ethical behavior. To help ensure our research and analysis are rigorous, objective, and nonpartisan, we subject our research publications to a robust and exacting quality-assurance process; avoid both the appearance and reality of financial and other conflicts of interest through staff training, project screening, and a policy of mandatory disclosure; and pursue transparency in our research engagements through our commitment to the open publication of our research findings and recommendations, disclosure of the source of funding of published research, and policies to ensure intellectual independence. For more information, visit www.rand.org/about/principles.

RAND's publications do not necessarily reflect the opinions of its research clients and sponsors.

About This Report

RAND Project Air Force was tasked with developing a new capability for planners: an early warning system that alerts policymakers when a subgroup of Air Force military members is at risk for future shortages. The goal of the research project was to develop an initial prediction prototype tool that can be used to alert decisionmakers of emerging problems and thus allow them enough time to consider adjusting accession and retention policies before shortages occur. In this report we first define the features and indicators that inform retention outcomes. We then describe a series of models we developed to help predict retention outcomes. Finally, we discuss a prototype tool that can be used to operationalize the information produced by the system.

This report should be of interest to decisionmakers responsible for policies aimed at retaining certain populations of Air Force members, as well as those responsible for policies affected by retention, such as recruiting, training, and promotions. More broadly, the research will be of interest to those who study military manpower and personnel issues.

The research reported here was commissioned by the Directors of Force Development (AF/A1D) and Military Force Management Policy (AF/A1P) and conducted within the Workforce, Development, and Health Program of RAND Project AIR FORCE as part of a fiscal year 2020 project entitled "Early Warning System for Negative Trends in Servicemember Retention."

RAND Project AIR FORCE

RAND Project AIR FORCE (PAF), a division of the RAND Corporation, is the Department of the Air Force's (DAF's) federally funded research and development center for studies and analyses, supporting both the United States Air Force and the United States Space Force. PAF provides the DAF with independent analyses of policy alternatives affecting the development, employment, combat readiness, and support of current and future air, space, and cyber forces. Research is conducted in four programs: Strategy and Doctrine; Force Modernization and Employment; Workforce, Development, and Health; and Resource Management. The research reported here was prepared under contract FA7014-16-D-1000.

This report documents work originally shared with the DAF on September 22, 2020. The draft report, issued on September 30, 2020, was reviewed by formal peer reviewers and DAF subject-matter experts.

Additional information about PAF is available on our website: www.rand.org/paf/

Contents

Figures

Tables

Summary

Issue

RAND Project Air Force was tasked with developing a new capability for planners: a retention early warning system (REWS) that alerts policymakers when a subgroup of Air Force military members is at risk for future shortages. The goal of the research project was to develop a forecasting model for retention, operationalized within a prototype decision-support application, that can alert decisionmakers of emerging problems and thus allow them enough time to consider adjusting accession and retention policies before shortages occur.

Approach

Our overall approach to designing the system drew on widely used paradigms for solving data science problems. These paradigms emphasize understanding the business problem, drawing on a wide array of data sources and types, testing several flexible prediction approaches to optimize performance, and operationalizing the information for decisionmaking. To inform our understanding of the data sources that would be desirable for this application, we also performed an extensive review of the turnover literature, identified gaps in existing data collection, and made recommendations to address them.

Findings

- The Air Force has access to rich historical information on many factors that the established research literature links to turnover. Further, the structure of the Air Force personnel system captures additional information beyond what a civilian employer would have access to, including precise information on when members become eligible to separate and when separation appears imminent.
- The most significant gap in turnover-related information available to REWS is the lack of information on member attitudes and perceptions. Possible sources for this information exist, but their frequency is not optimal for detecting negative trends that could affect retention.
- Machine learning (ML) algorithms can increase the accuracy of individual-level predictions, and these improvements result in more accurate group-level estimates for separation rates. The full models used dozens of variables from multiple sources, yet far simpler models that used ten variables that are already available to the Air Force also performed extremely well.
- The REWS decision workflow operationalizes these predictions so that various Air Force planners can generate customizable warnings, understand potential drivers, and assess the policy response required to preempt emerging problems. Figure S.1 shows an example visualization from the application that allows planners to see the impact of policies on the

REWS predictions. In the left panel, predicted retention (shown in teal/blue) in years six and 20 for intelligence specialties falls below the three-year moving average for these same specialties (solid red line). The right panel shows that it would require a 13-percent increase in retention to fully mitigate these gaps, which would be more than ten times the size of the effect of raising the Selective Reenlistment Bonus multiplier (Joffrion and Wozny, 2015).

Recommendations

- Feedback from human resources decisionmakers should guide REWS refinements.
- Alterations to retention survey data collection could enhance Air Force planning capabilities to anticipate negative trends.
- Simplified data inputs offer a way to refresh predictions with minimal resources while longer-term efforts improve data inputs, model accuracy, and functionality.

Figure S.1. Policy Impact Example for Intelligence Specialties

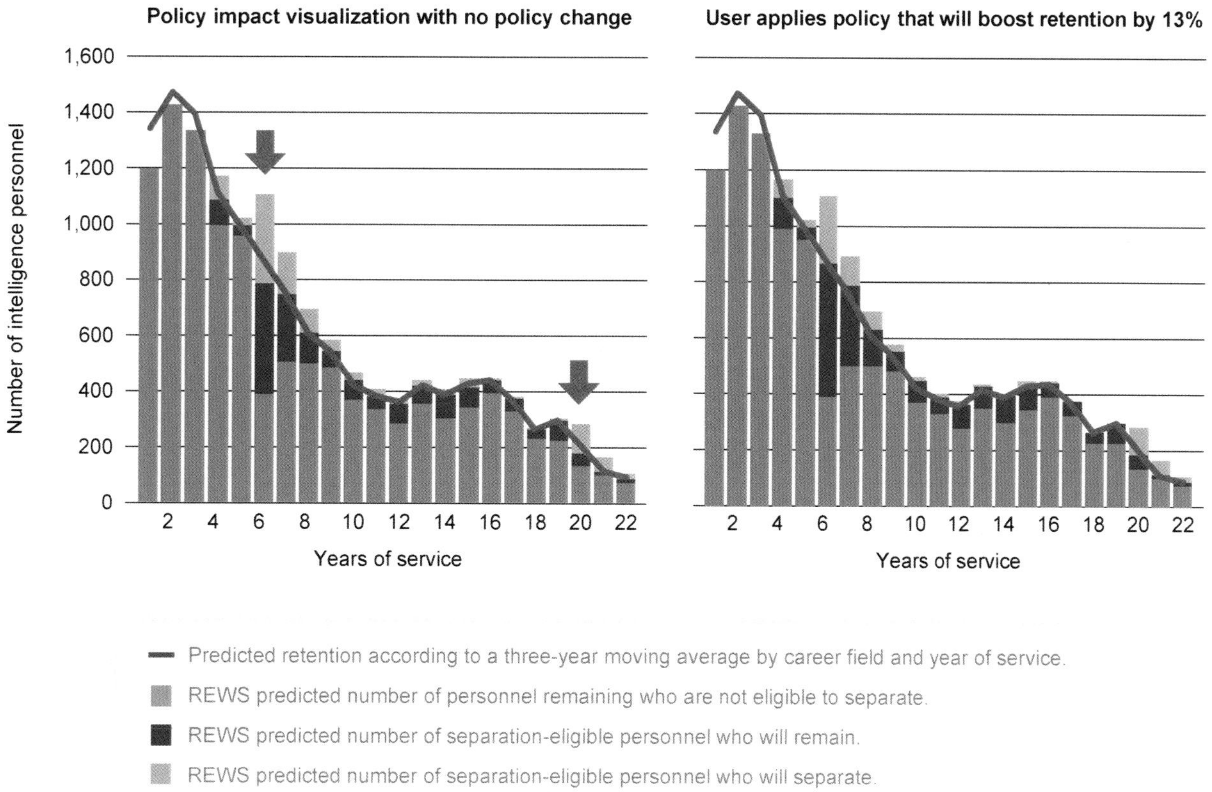

Policy impact visualization with no policy change
User applies policy that will boost retention by 13%
Number of intelligence personnel
1,600
1,400
1,200
1,000
800
600
400
200
0
2 4 6 8 10 12 14 16 18 20 22
Years of service
Predicted retention according to a three-year moving average by career field and year of service.
REWS predicted number of personnel remaining who are not eligible to separate.
REWS predicted number of separation-eligible personnel who will remain.
REWS predicted number of separation-eligible personnel who will separate.

Acknowledgments

We are grateful to our research co-sponsors, Russell Frasz and Brig Gen Troy Dunn, as well as Lisa Truesdale, for their continued support for this project. We also appreciate the help of action officers in within A1, including Lt Col Renee Thuotte, Lt Col Sherry Graham, and Col Justin Joffrion. We thank members of the Headquarters Air Force analytic staff for their feedback in developing the application: Lt Col Jeromie Shoulders, Capt Sean Ritter, Capt Stefan Zavislan, 1st Lt Lauren Bramblett, and Capt Morgan Mitchell. We appreciate our RAND teammates who provided counsel and assisted with data as part of the project, including Lou Mariano, Elliott Grant, Tiffany Berglund, Hannah Acheson-Field, Paul Emslie, and John Crown. We also thank Cord Thomas and Perry Firoz for their assistance making the application available to stakeholders. Finally, we are grateful to Nelson Lim for creating the concept for this project and to Ray Conley for his support and feedback throughout the process.

Abbreviations

3Y Ave	three-year average
ACS	American Community Survey
ADSC	active duty service commitment
AF/A1	Deputy Chief of Staff for Manpower, Personnel, and Services
AF/A1D	Directorate of Force Development
AF/A1P	Directorate for Force Management Policy
AF/A1X	Directorate for Plans and Integration
AF/A3	Deputy Chief of Staff for Operations
AFFMS	Air Force Fitness Management System
AFPC	Air Force Personnel Center
AFSC	Air Force specialty code
AI	artificial intelligence
AUC	area under the curve
BMI	body mass index
CPS	Current Population Survey
DAF	Department of the Air Force
DCAPES	Deliberate and Crisis Action Planning and Execution Segment
DMDC	Defense Manpower Data Center
DRM	Dynamic Retention Model
FY	fiscal year
GLM	General Linear Model
HR	human resources
HRM	human resource management
KNN	K-Nearest Neighbors
MilPDS	Military Personnel Data System
ML	machine learning

MOC	military occupational classification
NB	Naïve Bayes
PERSTEMPO	personnel tempo
REWS	Retention Early Warning System
RF	Random Forest
RNN	Recurrent Neural Network
SOC	standard occupational classification
SRB	Selective Reenlistment Bonus
TDY	temporary duty
XGB	Extreme Gradient Boosting
YOS	year(s) of service

1. Introduction

Managing employee retention is important to any organization, but it is especially critical for the Air Force and other military services because they depend on human capital investments made within the organization to meet human resource (HR) needs. Maintaining adequate numbers of skilled personnel across the diverse spectrum of military occupations is a complex long-term planning problem that spans many organizations within the Air Force. This planning process would be impossible without stable retention patterns, so policymakers continuously manage retention through a robust structure of commitments, contracts, incentives, and other policies. For instance, contracts and commitments ensure that less than a third of active component personnel are eligible to leave in a given year, and planners can further influence decisions through an annual special and incentive pay budget of over $1 billion (Department of the Air Force, 2020).

Offices under the Deputy Chief of Staff for Manpower, Personnel, and Services (AF/A1) as well as the Deputy Chief of Staff for Operations (AF/A3) have invested in the development of a suite of decisionmaking tools to help grapple with force management decisions. Regarding retention specifically, the Directorate for Force Management Policy (AF/A1P) has invested in econometric retention models that inform compensation levels for pilots (Mattock et al., 2016), remotely piloted aircraft pilots (Hardison, Mattock, and Lytell, 2012), and most recently enlisted aviators (Tong et al., 2020). These variants of RAND's Dynamic Retention Model (DRM) can simulate future retention patterns for these populations under altered compensation and benefit policies.

Still, discussions with personnel planners and analysts in AF/A1 indicate that there remains a broader need for a more general retention forecasting capability to inform other HR planning decisions. Table 1.1 lists the subordinate offices in AF/A1, their missions, and some sample retention considerations for each office. In addition to managing compensation policies to try to engineer desired retention levels, AF/A1P must factor expected retention into accession and promotion targets while also monitoring retention for members with specific skills and experiences. Retention considerations are also central to the mission of the Directorate of Force Development (AF/A1D), as this office pursues its strategies for shaping the proper blend of talent, experience, and demographic diversity at all levels. In addition to these offices, Table 1.1 lists other subordinate organizations within AF/A1 that have a more subsidiary interest in retention. Any requests for retention-related analyses to support decisionmaking would fall to a subordinate office within the Directorate for Plans and Integration (AF/A1X). Further, entities outside of AF/A1 that play a role in HR planning, such as career field functional authorities and managers and development teams, could benefit from access to retention predictions that are sufficiently customizable to their needs.

Table 1.1. Retention Considerations for Deputy Chief of Staff for Manpower, Personnel, and Services Subordinate Offices

Office	Mission	Retention Considerations
Directorate of Senior Leader Management (AF/A1L)	Advises on military and civilian senior personnel matters	• Minimize the loss of highly qualified senior leaders to competitive corporate markets
Directorate of Force Development (AF/A1D)	Develops airmen through developmental, education, and career mentorship programs; improves Air Force service culture through diversity and inclusion strategies and initiatives	• Identify and address demographic disparities in servicemember retention • Develop policies to retain servicemembers with critical knowledge, skills, abilities, and experiences
Directorate of Military Force Management Policy (AF/A1P)	Develops policies to shape and balance the force through recruiting, accessions, retirement/ separations, promotions/evaluations, and other personnel elements	• Set accession targets to replace projected losses • Calculate the number of promotions to replace projected losses in each grade • Develop policies to retain servicemembers with critical knowledge, skills, abilities, and experiences
Directorate of Services (AF/A1S)	Serves as a principal advisor for the Air Force Services program and provides advice and counsel to major commands on programs under their jurisdiction	• Examine the relationship between base resources and programs, geographical location, and servicemember retention
Directorate of Plans and Integration (AF/A1X)	Ensures that AF/A1's strategic goals are aligned with the President's Management Agenda, the Office of the Secretary of Defense's Defense Planning Guidance, and the Air Force's Annual Planning and Programming Guidance	• Plan and program for Air Force endstrength • Incorporate separation forecasts into career field sustainment charts • Prospectively identify critical shortages by Air Force specialty code (AFSC), skills, or years of service (YOS) arising from retention trends
Directorate of Integrated Resilience (A1Z)	Responsible for contributing to mission readiness through Air Force–wide policy and program oversight for violence prevention and response	• Identify trends in selected types of separations across deployment experiences, career fields, and demographic factors
Directorate of Equal Opportunity (A1Q)	Responsible for developing equal opportunity and human relations policy	• Identify trends in servicemember retention by demographic category • Develop policies to address demographic disparities in servicemember retention
Directorate of Manpower, Organization and Resources (AF/A1M)	Defines Air Force manpower requirements	• Incorporate separation trends into workforce mix policy and resourcing

SOURCE: RAND analysis based on U.S. Air Force Deputy Chief of Staff, Manpower, Personnel, and Services, 2019.

In consultation with the project sponsor, we established goals for creating a system to address AF/A1's identified capability gap. The system should

- present general retention information flexibly for different personnel categories that might be relevant to the domains of various offices or organizational levels
- predict across different time horizons depending on the relevant planning or policy decision

- systematically capture relevant information from multiple data sources
- easily ingest new information as it becomes available
- provide a customizable warning to planners based on relevant risk criteria.

The purpose of our project was to explore methods for an initial capability and create a prototype application to enable HR policymakers to better predict, and therefore anticipate, retention challenges. The analogy of an early warning radar system is useful—one that provides *lower*-resolution information about targets across a greater distance. The early warning radar cues other radar systems that then provide more precise tracking information. Personnel planners desired a retention early warning system (REWS) that would complement existing capabilities by enabling them to scan their workforce categories and identify areas that are at risk of unanticipated retention challenges in the coming years.

Research Approach

The purpose of some types of HR research is to arm decisionmakers with policy options and comparisons of the effects of those options. One example is research done to predict how individuals will respond to various compensation packages that the Air Force offers (Asch, Mattock, and Hosek, 2013). Although DRM is a powerful model to answer questions regarding compensation and retention, it is structurally complex and narrowly tailored.

In keeping with the comparison to an early warning radar system, we avoided focusing too much on particular policies in order to keep the capability general enough to be useful to a broad community of HR decisionmakers. We based our approach on research techniques for extracting operational information from data, sometimes referred to as *data mining*, or *knowledge discovery in databases* (Mariscal, Marbán, and Fernández, 2010). These techniques emphasize a workflow that begins by understanding the business problem and available data before engaging in an iterative process of engineering a system to support decisionmaking needs. In data-mining applications, the precise data inputs and model structure are of lesser importance as compared with the predictive performance of the resulting system.

Figure 1.1 depicts an example data-mining process flowchart for applying data science techniques to address HR operational needs (Tambe, Cappelli, and Yakubovich, 2019).[1] The **first step** is to identify the HR operation and associated objectives, goals, and success criteria, which we have done in the previous section. The **second step** is to collect data. In the commercial context, data may include demographic factors, job performance, or other digital traces related to email and internet activity. The structure inherent in managing retention in the military offers a variety of additional factors that could be useful, such as contracts and service

---

[1] The process shown in Figure 1.1 is a simplification of other established data science frameworks like the Cross-Industry Standard Process for Data Mining (CRISP-DM); see Chapman et al., 2000.

commitments, physical fitness scores, promotion timing, and operational activities. The **third step** is to create a model that links available data about an individual to whether or not he or she remains in a job. In our military setting, this means linking historical data about an individual officer or enlisted member to whether he or she remained on active service. In this stage, it is a common practice to test a variety of machine learning (ML) algorithms and choose the method that achieves the best performance. The operational system can then use the top-performing model to generate predictions on new individuals whose future separation patterns are unknown. The **final step** is to use insights gained from the previous steps to improve HR operations. In our specific application, improvements come from warnings that future retention is either negative or unexpected for a specific Air Force subpopulation.

Figure 1.1. Steps in Applying Data Mining to Human Resources Operations

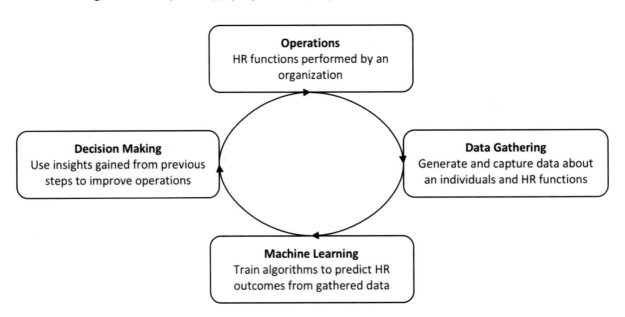

SOURCE: Adapted from Tambe, Cappelli, and Yakubovich, 2019.

Outline of This Report

The structure of this report follows the process model in Figure 1.1. Chapters 2 and 3 focus on different aspects of data gathering. Chapter 2 summarizes the results of our research and identifies potential factors that could relate to retention, while Chapter 3 summarizes the available data and highlights gaps where unmeasured factors could potentially improve retention predictions in the future. Chapter 4 focuses on the ML stage in Figure 1.1 and discusses modeling approaches and performance. Chapter 5 covers the decisionmaking phase by focusing on how HR managers can use model predictions to generate warnings of unanticipated retention challenges. Chapter 6 concludes the report by discussing next steps for further development and implementation of the system.

2. What Information Is Most Relevant to Predicting Retention?

We begin the data-gathering phase of the project by examining the research literature on employee turnover and military retention with three main goals. First, we review established turnover frameworks to inform the REWS model design. Second, we consider existing empirical work on factors that predict retention and associated data sources to help guide our own search for data. This work could also inform the process of feature engineering, which is the art of presenting information to the model in a way that makes it easier for the model to find relationships (Allaire, 2018). Third, while current efforts can use only data that are already collected and accessible, prior research could highlight gaps where Air Force data systems do not capture important factors that relate to turnover. We distilled this information into our own retention framework, which we describe in this chapter.

Conceptual Frameworks Describing Turnover

Literature addressing factors that influence retention in private-sector organizations tends to focus on turnover, which is "the percent[age] of employees leaving an organization" (Phillips and Edwards, 2009, p. 29). Broadly, literature distinguishes between whether or not turnover is "avoidable" or "unavoidable" from the standpoint of organizational management and, similarly, whether or not turnover is "voluntary" or "nonvoluntary" on the part of employees (Figure 2.1). Avoidable turnover is turnover that could have been prevented by an organization—for example, when an employee leaves due to conflict with a bad manager—whereas unavoidable turnover is turnover that the organization likely could not have prevented—for instance, when an employee moves for family reasons or retires. Voluntary turnover means an employee initiates turnover by, for example, taking a better job opportunity, whereas involuntary turnover is initiated by the employer, as in the case of employee layoffs.

Typically, an organization has the most control over turnover that is both voluntary and avoidable because there are typically more opportunities for intervening in support of employee retention. This distinction applies to the Air Force as well, as we discuss in the following chapters. Because Air Force programs and policies also affect members' nonwork lives to a greater extent than those of a typical civilian employer, Air Force HR managers might consider a broader range of circumstances to be avoidable than a civilian organization would.

Because a wide range of factors can affect an individual's decision to stay or go in any organization, conceptual frameworks in literature are helpful for grouping factors into broader thematic categories. Approaches for categorizing retention/turnover factors include levels of analysis, embeddedness, decisionmaking processes, and economic models.

Conceptual frameworks based on levels of analysis are valuable because they address the family and personal life factors, career factors, and work environment factors, as well as broader

Figure 2.1. Types of Turnover

		Organizational Control: Yes	Organizational Control: No
		Avoidable Employee exit could have been prevented	**Unavoidable** Employee exit could not have been prevented
Employee Control: Yes	**Voluntary** Employee decides to exit	**Voluntary/avoidable** • E.g., poor supervisor, compensation issues, poor work environment • AF context: pilot separating for airline position with better pay/stability	**Voluntary/unavoidable** • E.g., moving, going back to school, changing careers • AF context: separating voluntarily to pursue a career change irrespective of circumstances
Employee Control: No	**Involuntary** Organization initiates an employee's exit	**Involuntary/avoidable** • E.g., layoffs, performance issues, restructuring • AF context: force shaping to meet functional requirements or end	**Involuntary/unavoidable** • E.g., retirement, disability, death • AF context: retiring involuntarily for medical reasons

SOURCES: Allen, 2008; Phillips and Edwards, 2009.
NOTE: For an organization as large and diverse as the Air Force, it is difficult to imagine a voluntary separation that is completely unpreventable if the only goal is to retain one particular person. Rather, the table columns reflect the distinction between separations that are caused by policies that HR systems normally seek to optimize, while other voluntary losses are more idiosyncratic and not practically addressed by standard HR policies.

Air Force and military factors that can affect retention (Keller et al., 2018). Embeddedness models address the factors that make a person stay, or the "totality of forces that solidify staying in organizations" (Kiazad et al., 2015, p. 641). Key dimensions in these types of frameworks include formal and informal ties to others at work or in the community (links); one's compatibility with one's job and environment (fit); and what one forfeits (materially or psychologically) when one leaves the organization or communities (sacrifices). The value of such models lies in their relational perspective, through which they identify how social ties impact retention.

Decisionmaking process and motivation-focused frameworks focus on how employees make decisions about whether or not to stay in their organization. Several such models take a decision-tree approach to understanding an individual motivation to stay or leave an organization.[1] Similar models map out the degree to which employee expectations are met.[2] RAND's DRM (Mattock and Arkes, 2007; Mattock et al., 2016) is an example of a model that addresses decisionmaking by

---

[1] See Singh and Sharma (2015) for a review of employee turnover models from 1975 to 1995.

[2] These include the met expectation model (Porter and Steers, 1973); the turnover process model (Mobley, 1977); and the motivational forces model (Maertz and Griffeth, 2004).

highlighting pecuniary and other factors, such as Air Force policy, compensation, and benefits, as well as individual tastes for military service.

In order to assess the range of retention-relevant data that the Air Force currently collects and to inform recommendations for refinement, we pulled together elements from several of these conceptual models (including Hausknecht and Trevor, 2011; Hom, Allen, and Griffeth, 2020; Joseph et al. 2007). The resulting framework includes attempts to include a wide range of factors that are relevant to a Department of the Air Force (DAF) context. The conceptual framework shown in Figure 2.2 summarizes factors from the literature that contribute to collective turnover, meaning "the aggregate levels of employee departures that occur within groups, work units, or organizations" (Hausknecht and Trevor, 2011).

Figure 2.2. Conceptual Framework Summary

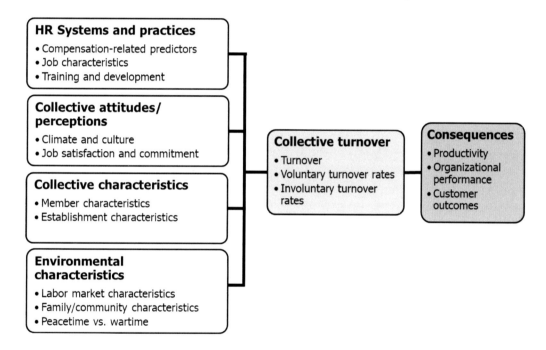

Retention Predictors and Types of Data

In this simple framework, antecedents (HR systems and practices, collective attitudes and perceptions, collective characteristics, and environmental characteristics) inform collective turnover, which in turn, informs organizational consequences (productivity, firm performance, and customer outcomes). Within the framework we incorporated factors from a range of literature sources.[3] Tables 2.1–2.4 list more detailed types of data within each broader category, which research has previously linked to retention.

---

[3] See Appendix D for a description of the literature review that informed the conceptual framework.

Table 2.1. Conceptual Framework Categories: Human Resources Systems and Practices

HR Systems and Practices	Description and Examples

Compensation-related predictors	Pay relative to the market
	    pay; cost of living allowances; other allowances; total monetary compensation
	Incentives
	    compensation/incentives for remote/dangerous work; retention bonus; performance rewards
	Benefits
	    paid time off, insurance, retirement/pension

Job characteristics	Work design and organization of work
	    adequate resources; skill requirements; type of tasks; number of procedures and regulations; opportunities for continuous learning; extent of self-direction
	Staffing/selection
	    role clarity; role conflict; role overload; staffing selectivity; staffing levels relative to workload; internal vs. external staffing; validated selection process
	Voice
	    participation-enhancing practices that increase employee discretion, autonomy, and control over work; ability to provide feedback including formal grievance processes, peer review systems, ombudsperson roles, or dispute resolution
	Downsizing or changes that impact morale

Training and development	Quality or amount of training provided to employees
	    availability of training/educational opportunities; opportunity to acquire new knowledge and skills; quality of training for job
	Promotion systems and recent promotions
	    actual promotions; availability of/assignment to key development positions; availability/timeliness of promotions/advancement opportunities; fairness of promotion system; communication regarding career-related/advancement information

Table 2.2. Conceptual Framework Categories: Collective Attitudes/Perceptions

Collective Attitudes/ Perceptions	Description and Examples
Climate and culture	Perceptions about the workplace and workplace norms psychological climate; job stress; sense of meaningfulness; supportiveness

Job satisfaction and commitment	Job satisfaction
	    job satisfaction level; job satisfaction change; enjoyment in serving in job; fulfillment from job; amount of operational and combat stress during deployments; meet expectations; meet cultural and ethnic needs; desire for challenging/useful work; sense of accomplishment; desire for autonomy
	Commitment
	    unemployment rate; economic growth or decline; skill shortage

Management/leadership/ supervision quality	Attitudes toward management/quality of management; supervisory satisfaction; attitudes toward senior executives/leaders

Collective Attitudes/ Perceptions	Description and Examples
	Allowance for innovation/creativity/openness to new ideas
	leader allowance for innovating/creativity; openness to new ideas
	Leader trust
	mentoring and mentorship
Organizational justice/ fairness	Amount of decisionmaking authority/autonomy
	Dispute resolution
	Perceptions of fairness (e.g., pay fairness)
	Fairness in career progression opportunities
Cohesiveness/ teamwork	Coworker satisfaction
	integration
	group camaraderie; mutual respect and support; peer group relations; trust group morale

Table 2.3. Conceptual Framework Categories: Collective Characteristics

Collective Characteristics	Description and Examples
Member characteristics	Demographics/workforce composition
	includes experience; age/average age; education/average education; gender; ethnicity/race; tenure/average tenure; experience concentration; percent female; percent full-time; start date
	Organization size
	size of group or unit; average number of employees
	Member behaviors
	withdrawal behaviors (absenteeism, lateness); organizational citizenship behaviors
	Member qualities
	personality attributes (agreeableness; conscientiousness; coping; emotional stability; internal motivation; openness to experience); goals and values; cognitive ability
	Member health
	general health; physical well-being; emotional exhaustion; depression
	Shocks
	job shocks (personal, work-related, or opportunity-related events that precipitate turnover decisions); death of friend/family member; sexual harassment; sexual assault
Establishment characteristics	Size, age, and tenure of organization
	Quality of location
	organizational prestige; site quality; quality, cost, and convenience of health care services; quality of schools available for children; weather; available entertainment; political climate; religious climate; city size; adult educational opportunities; housing quality and availability
	Stability
	move timing; frequency of moves; number of locations
	Accessibility of information relevant to career

Table 2.4. Conceptual Framework Categories: Environmental Characteristics

Environmental Characteristics	Description and Examples

Labor market characteristics	Macroeconomic indicators
	    unemployment rate; economic growth or decline; skill shortage
	Alternative opportunities
	    alternative job availability; attraction of alternative job; career opportunities; comparison of alternative job to present job; civilian sector job and retirement benefits; hiring in specific sector; shortage of special skills; confidence in obtaining a job; probability of finding an alternative job; job security

Family/community characteristics	Quality of life
	    opportunities for spouse/significant other's career and education
	Spouse/significant other or family satisfaction/support
	    benefits that are instrumental to the overall well-being of families; communication with family during job-related travel; freedom to choose location or position; family's opinion on staying or leaving; impact on significant other/family well-being; impact on ability to start/maintain personal relationships; personal/family support
	Work-life balance and tempo
	    advance notice of work-related travel and moves; amount of personal and family time; workload/number of work hours; number, length, predictability of work-related travel to remote/dangerous locations; number of nights away from home; length of average work week

Working environment	Setting remoteness; separation from family; hazardousness; combat zone or garrison

The conceptual framework helps to ensure that Air Force retention modelers consider the full range of factors. Our literature review included several analyses of military retention that incorporated job characteristics (under HR systems and practices) or member characteristics (under collective characteristics). Further, as discussed in the introduction, a body of research has focused on military compensation, as well as labor market characteristics for certain populations (such as airline hiring for pilots). Previous studies have also focused specifically on the tempo of operations (under environmental characteristics). Notably, our review highlights the collective attitudes and perceptions category as a potential untapped resource for military retention, as very few military studies specifically measure these factors and link them to retention behaviors, despite the support for the linkage in studies of civilian organizations. The following chapter discusses the available data for the current study, while using the framework as a lens to understand the scope of current data collection and suggest possible areas for refinement.

3. Available Sources of Information for Predicting Air Force Retention

Whereas Chapter 2 examined factors from literature that have been shown to influence turnover, this chapter examines the information available to REWS for the Air Force population. The conceptual framework developed from literature serves as a guide because it identifies and organizes factors that previous studies have shown to contribute to individuals' decisions about whether to stay with an organization or whether to leave. After reviewing available Air Force data, we conclude the chapter with an assessment of gaps where the framework highlights important information unavailable to REWS.

Data Sources

The Air Force gathers data on individuals beginning with recruitment and continuing through separation (or retirement). These data are collected and recorded for different purposes by offices responsible for a variety of Air Force policies and entered into different personnel systems. When combined, these data provide an opportunity to explore associations between a large number of individual, job, and organizational factors and annual retention behaviors. We started by compiling known sources of data on individual members, Air Force policies, and external factors hypothesized to impact retention behavior. Table 3.1 depicts a high-level summary of the types of data, potential data sources, and the availability of data for REWS. In some cases, the table depicts a type of data as having "partial" availability, which means that the data source was available to the effort, but that the data source does not completely capture the key data dimension. For example, the Military Personnel Data System (MilPDS) promotion data contain some information on enlisted and officer performance, but they do not capture narratives from performance evaluations. Not all available data sources listed were used in the final REWS model.[1]

Using the conceptual framework presented in Chapter 2 and available data sources, we reviewed potential predictors contained in Air Force personnel systems and created two relational databases—one containing historical individual-level variables for all officers hypothesized to be related to retention and one for enlisted personnel. Appendix A provides further details about how these variables were defined and derived, as well as the completeness of measures across all records.

---

[1] In some instances, data did not improve the model; see Chapter 4 for a description of how REWS was developed.

Table 3.1. Potential Data Types and Sources

Types of Data	Potential Sources	Available for the Current Version of REWS (Yes/No/Partial)
Administrative (e.g., years served, gender, AFSC)	MilPDS, officer and enlisted promotion	Yes
Performance	MilPDS, officer and enlisted promotion	Partial
Pay	Defense Finance and Accounting System data maintained by the Defense Manpower Data Center (DMDC)	No; however, some information can be inferred from other sources
Fitness test results	Air Force Fitness Management System (AFFMS)	Yes
Absences/reasons	Duty status codes from MilPDS	Yes
History of deployments/deployment length	Deliberate and Crisis Action Planning and Execution Segments	Yes
Family characteristics/satisfaction with military life	MilPDS; surveys of military spouses	Partial
Responses to quality-of-life surveys	Total Force Climate Survey	No
Responses to unit climate surveys	Defense Equal Opportunity Management Institute Organizational Climate Survey	No
Conditions in national, regional, and occupational labor markets	American Community Survey; Bureau of Labor Statistics	Yes
Historical data on eligibility and acceptance of retention incentives	MilPDS and Air Staff A1 records	Partial
Historical data on separations resulting from force shaping/eligibility and acceptance of retention incentives	MilPDS and Air Staff A1 records	Partial
Personnel tempo (PERSTEMPO)[a] information such as time away and activity levels	PERSTEMPO database (maintained by AF/A1XD)	No
Indications of workload	Career field manning in Manpower Programming and Execution System; Total Force Climate Survey	Partial

[a] PERSTEMPO and deployment are similar concepts. According to statutory definitions, PERSTEMPO refers to any circumstance that prevents a member from spending off-duty time in his or her residence, while deployments specifically refer to support for training exercises or operations (Congressional Research Service, 2020).

Of the potentially vast number of predictor variables, we retained ones that might reasonably be expected to affect retention decisions (Table 3.2). These variables provided some coverage for three of the four categories presented in the conceptual model: HR systems and practices, collective characteristics, and environmental characteristics. Notably, we were unable to identify any variables that measured collective attitudes and perceptions.

Table 3.2. Conceptual Framework Categories and Corresponding Variables

Category	Variable[a]
HR Systems and practices	
Compensation-related predictors	Selective Reenlistment Bonus (SRB) zone; SRB multiplier (E)
Job characteristics	Core AFSC; duty AFSC; days deployed in previous 30 months; months deployed in previous fiscal year (FY); months on temporary duty (TDY) in previous FY; recency of previous deployment (E & O)
Training and development	Promotion status (O)
	Skill level; enlisted performance report rating; promotion fitness examination score; skills knowledge test score (E)
	Medal count (E & O)
Collective attitudes/perceptions	
Climate and culture	(No data available)
Job satisfaction and commitment	(No data available)
Management/leadership/ supervision quality	(No data available)
Organizational justice/fairness	(No data available)
Cohesiveness/teamwork	(No data available)
Collective characteristics	
Member characteristics	Active duty service commitment (ADSC) source indicators (E & O)
	Commission source; distinguished graduate (O)
	Age; education level; gender; race/ethnicity; religion; rank; YOS (E & O)
	Duty status; misconduct during previous year; separation effective date; separation eligibility; maximum ADSC complete; days until maximum ADSC complete; nondeployable for administrative, legal, medical or retainability (E & O)
	Re-enlistment eligibility; enlistment category; enlistment term; days until enlistment term complete; enlistment term complete (E)
	Fitness test scores (aerobic; pushup; sit-up; abdominal circumference); fitness test exemptions (composite; aerobic; pushup; sit-up; abdominal circumference); body mass index (BMI); months sick in previous FY (E & O)
	Years voluntary and involuntary force shaping is in effect (E & O)
Establishment characteristics	Assignment location; end strength; percentage females by AFSC; cohort separation rate during previous year; 3-year average (3Y Ave) separation rate for AFSC and YOS; 3Y Ave separation rate among separation-eligible individuals for AFSC and YOS (E & O)
Environmental characteristics	
Labor market characteristics	Median household income by zip code; unemployment by zip code; median compensation by zip code; national median wage; national median compensation by occupation; national unemployment by occupation; monthly national unemployment (E & O)
Family/community characteristics	Marital status; married to military spouse; number of minor dependents; number of adult dependents (E & O)
Working environment	(No data available)

[a] (E) denotes variables present in enlisted cohort; (O) denotes variables present in officer cohort. We allowed for the possibility that variables could fit more than one conceptual category. We also considered how combinations of variables could be used to address a given category.

Improved Survey Methods Could Close Collective Attitudes and Perceptions Gap

Despite the existence of data from several sources, we were unable to derive variables that pertained to the category of collective attitudes and perceptions. The Air Force Personnel Center (AFPC) does collect attitudinal data from several surveys. The Military Career Decisions Survey is administered every two years and assesses factors related to retention. The Military Exit Survey is sent out multiple times a year to groups of airmen with a date of separation on file. Every two to three years, the Air Force conducts a Total Force Climate Survey, which collects information on member perceptions of their work environment and organizational climate (Salomon, 2018). Unit commanders also conduct organizational climate surveys after assuming command and periodically thereafter (U.S. Air Force, 2013). Other than the Military Career Decisions Survey, which seeks a representative sample of the active duty force,[2] the other efforts solicit responses from all personnel within the respective scope. We tried to acquire data from these surveys for this project with the assumption that some variables derived from that data (particularly satisfaction measures) could fill in this gap in the data and inform the REWS model, but we were unable to access it in time.

While the Career Decisions Survey provides AFPC with a valuable snapshot of data about airmen attitudes, the fact that data are captured every two years limits the degree to which they can contribute to the goal of continuously measuring and monitoring retention trends. Changes to the timing and design of the Career Decisions Survey could enable it to better capture attitudinal data that can shed light on retention trends while taking into account the potential burden on respondents. We refer to the Current Population Survey (CPS) as an example of a survey with features that mirror our design recommendations (U.S. Census Bureau, 2019).

First, we recommend administering a version of the Career Decisions survey multiple times a year to better monitor trends in attitudes and behaviors, as well as responses to policy changes. For instance, CPS is administered monthly for the purpose of producing timely labor market statistics. By administering a repeated cross-sectional survey on a more frequent basis, AFPC can produce more timely information for decisionmakers as changes unfold.

Second, in addition to continuing the use of stratified sampling, AFPC could consider using a quasi-panel approach similar to the approach used in CPS. In CPS, households are included for four consecutive months; they are then out for eight, and then back in for four more months (U.S. Census Bureau, 2019). Respondents are then removed from the sample so that they are not surveyed again and again. The purpose of surveying households in this 4-8-4 quasi-panel pattern is to allow for some degree of continuity of data over time without overburdening respondents.

---

[2] AFPC sends out the Career Decisions Survey to approximately 230,000 airmen. They take steps to make sure their survey sample is proportionate to subsets of the DAF population.

It also allows for analyses to look at changes in individual statuses over time. For AFPC, a quasi-panel approach could allow for additional analysis opportunities while balancing potential respondent burden.

Third, survey content can be edited to help reduce potential burden on airmen if the frequency of surveys is increased. For example, in CPS, a set of core questions is used monthly with supplemental questions that are administered during only one of the months every year.[3] This type of core-plus-supplement design would allow AFPC to continue to collect detailed biennial data, while also generating more frequent and actionable information on collective attitudes that relate to retention. These changes could support AFPC's current survey approach, while providing a way to better track airmen attitudes over time without overburdening them.

Adopting a more complex survey design at a higher frequency for the Career Decisions Survey would generate better retention information for decisionmaking, but it would also raise the administration cost substantially. The CPS reaches its sampling target each month of 60,000 households by utilizing an army of 2,700 part-time field representatives to conduct telephone and in-person interviews. As a result, the response rate in recent years has been better than 85 percent (U.S. Census Bureau, 2019). To achieve CPS-like capabilities, AFPC would need to develop a sampling design and frequency that meets its decision needs and find a staffing solution (e.g., deputized unit representatives) to increase contact points with respondents.

Summary

This chapter describes the range of data sources available and the sources used in the REWS model. We also identify a gap in data addressing airmen attitudes and perceptions related to turnover and retention. Although AFPC has at least one tool, the Career Decisions Survey, that assesses attitudinal data, we were unable to acquire that data for this project. However, the biennial frequency of the Career Decisions Survey would have likely limited its usefulness in detecting the sorts of changes in attitudes and perceptions that would affect retention forecasts. Changes to the design and administration of the Career Decisions Survey could provide more valuable inputs that are currently missing from the other data sources used in the REWS model. Our recommendations include administering a shorter, more frequent version of the survey and the use of carefully designed sampling procedures to acquire more frequent attitudinal data without overburdening airmen. By making changes to survey data collection, AFPC has an opportunity to get more from their survey data with regard to tracking retention trends.

---

[3] For example, the Annual Social and Economic Supplement to the CPS collects additional data on "family characteristics, household composition, marital status, educational attainment, health insurance coverage, foreign-born population, prior year's income from all sources, work experience, receipt of noncash benefit, poverty, program participation, and geographic mobility" (U.S. Census Bureau, 2019, p. 15).

4. Modeling Approaches and Performance Levels

This chapter describes the ML phase of the data science process. In contrast to more traditional workforce planning activities, applying data science to HR requires adopting a different perspective and new methods for learning from data (Breiman, 2001). Traditionally, organizational researchers would select a limited number of variables thought to relate to the outcome of interest (i.e., separation) and then attempt to infer the underlying causal model linking variables to the outcome. Researchers would evaluate the causal model in terms of its ability to account for existing data and, to a lesser extent, its ability to predict future outcomes.

In contrast, ML methods may take a vast number of variable inputs. Rather than trying to infer a causal model, these methods seek to learn a "black-box" function that maximizes the accuracy of predictions about future outcomes. This shift involves a trade-off between flexibility and interpretability. Given enough data, ML methods with a high degree of flexibility may make very accurate predictions, yet it may be hard to understand how they arrive at those predictions.

We chose to model separations at the individual level, because this was the only way to meet the design requirement that predictions could be flexibly aggregated for the variety of personnel categories that might pertain to the missions of different organizations. Servicemembers' annual retention decisions result in one of two outcomes: separate from the active component or remain. Predicting retention decisions is, therefore, a classification problem with two classes.[1] Given the variables listed in Table 3.2, can a model accurately predict whether an individual will separate or remain? We trained multiple models using historical values of the predictor variables for individuals and their retention decisions. We then used the fitted models to predict future separations for individuals when only the values of the predictor variables are known.

Current Practice for Predicting Separations

From FY 2005 to FY 2019, the percentage of officers separating from active duty (including retirements) on an annual basis ranged from 6 to 13 percent, and the percentage of enlisted personnel separating ranged from 10 to 13 percent.[2] Separation rates vary across officer and enlisted subpopulations. For example, separation rates are near zero for early-career officers bound by initial active duty service commitments (ADSCs); they increase for mid-career officers who have satisfied the initial ADSC; and then they decrease as officers approach eligibility for

---

[1] A servicemember may also decide to leave the active component and enter the reserve component. In this case, the classification problem would involve three class labels: remains in the active component, enters the reserve component, and departs from the total force.

[2] Values derived from records extracted from MilPDS.

16

retirement.[3] Likewise, separation rates are lower for enlisted personnel bound by ADSC and enlistment contracts, and they are higher for individuals who are eligible for separation or retirement.

Discussions with Air Force personnel analysts revealed that standard practice for forecasting future retention is to calculate three-year moving averages by AFSC and YOS. These averages are then used as inputs to major personnel planning processes, such as determining required numbers of accessions and setting promotion allocations to replace projected losses. Three-year moving averages may approximate the standard retention profile for a given career field, but they fail to capture the effects of HR systems and practices, collective attitudes and perceptions, collective characteristics, and environmental characteristics known to influence retention decisions.

In this chapter, we use ML techniques to predict servicemembers' separation decisions based on data contained in available personnel records and other data sources. The statistical models we develop go beyond 3Y Aves in that they account for the effects of many other variables identified using the conceptual framework described in Chapter 2.

Data Science Approach for Predicting Servicemember Separation Decisions

We created analytical files with annual snapshots of active duty officers and enlisted personnel from FY 2005 to FY 2019.[4] The officer and enlisted files contained 107 and 111 predictor variables, respectively. The individual predictor variables include indicators and metrics associated with the variable descriptions in Table 3.2. The outcome of interest was whether or not the servicemember separated from active duty in a given year.

We implemented six classification methods: General Linear Models (GLM), K-Nearest Neighbors (KNN), Naïve Bayes (NB), Random Forest (RF), Extreme Gradient Boosting (XGB), and Recurrent Neural Networks (RNN). The methods reflect a mix of traditional and contemporary approaches for classification and are described in Appendix B. We compared the performance of the methods to one another and to the performance of a 3Y Ave within AFSC and YOS.

To evaluate the models, we selected a test year (e.g., FY 2019) and then trained the models using data from the previous ten years (e.g., FY 2009–FY 2018). This is akin to the task faced by

---

[3] An open question is whether the transition to a blended retirement system will change these traditional retention patterns. The Air Force can theoretically reproduce these historical patterns under a blended retirement system, but the actual outcome depends on how the Air Force implements aspects of the system, such as continuation pay multipliers (Asch, Mattock, and Hosek, 2017).

[4] This resulted in a total of 975,207 person-year records in the officer file, and 3,912,822 person-year records in the enlisted file.

Air Staff personnel analysts: Given everything that is known about an officer up until the current time (i.e., up to and including FY 2018), how likely is it that the individual will separate during the coming year? Data from the coming year cannot be used to improve predictions because, in practice, those data will not be available at the time when predictions must be made. For example, an officer's performance on the Air Force Physical Fitness Test during FY 2020 is not yet known at the start of FY 2020, when the model must predict whether the officer will separate during that year. We repeated this training process five times while varying the test year from FY 2015 to FY 2019.[5] Figure 4.1 summarizes the scheme for model training and testing.

Figure 4.1. Machine Learning Training and Testing Protocol

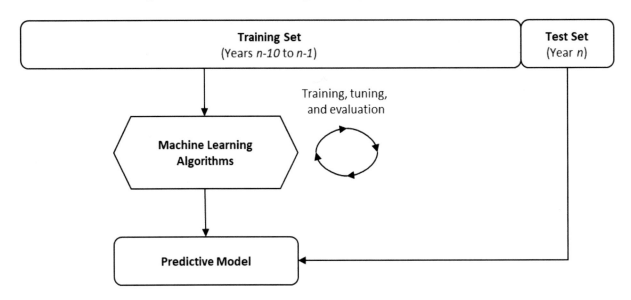

We evaluated the models using four metrics: accuracy, precision, recall, and area under the curve (AUC).[6] To calculate the first three metrics (accuracy, precision, and recall), we predicted whether each person in the test data would separate based solely on whether the ML model gave the person at least a 50-percent chance of separation (i.e., it is more likely than not that he or she will separate). Accuracy is the overall percentage of predictions that match outcomes; it captures the tendency for the model to correctly predict separations. Recall is the percentage of actual separations that the model predicts. Precision is the percentage of predicted separations that actually separated. Together, precision and recall illustrate the trade-off between correctly

---

[5] This also entailed shifting the training range to exclude the test year.

[6] The "curve" in AUC refers to the receiver operator characteristic curve, which plots the false-positive rate of a model against its true-positive rate for varying decision thresholds. AUC provides a general measure of accuracy that does not require a particular threshold, such as 50 percent, to determine whether the model predicts that a person will separate. A common rule of thumb is to reject classifiers with an AUC of below 0.80 (Kotu and Deshpande, 2019).

identifying more of the servicemembers who will separate (recall) without incorrectly identifying servicemembers who will not (precision). Finally, AUC describes the probability that the classifier will rank a randomly chosen individual who separates more highly than a person who does not. AUC tells how much the model is capable of distinguishing between those who separate and those who do not. Additional details about the models, training, and test procedures are contained in Appendix B.

Results

Predicting Separations in the Current Year

Table 4.1 compares the performance of the statistical and ML methods for officers and enlisted personnel. Higher values indicate better performance. The base rates for individuals remaining in the force are high (92.8 percent for officers and 90.0 percent for enlisted). The accuracy of a "naïve" model that predicts that nobody will separate equals these values. Thus, the base rates establish a lower bound for evaluating model accuracy. Accuracy exceeded this lower bound for several methods and was highest for RF and XGB. The other metrics followed the same pattern: RF and XGB had among the highest recall (i.e., the percentage of actual separations that were predicted), precision (i.e., the percentage of predicted separations that actually separated), and AUC (i.e., the ability to differentiate between individuals who separate and those who do not). The remaining methods (3Y Ave, GLM, KNN, NB, and RNN) all had significantly lower values for at least one of the performance metrics. RF and

Table 4.1. Model Results for One-Year Predictions

Sample	Method	Accuracy (Percentage)	Recall (Percentage)	Precision (Percentage)	AUC
Officer	3Y Ave	92.7	1.7	45.2	0.76
	GLM	93.3	53.3	53.6	0.88
	KNN	93.6	11.7	97.9	0.90
	NB	89.9	48.1	35.5	0.84
	RF	96.1	49.0	94.1	0.93
	XGB	96.1	52.0	90.1	0.94
	RNN	96.0	46.3	96.0	0.91
Enlisted	3Y Ave	90.2	4.4	67.8	0.75
	GLM	91.7	45.4	61.8	0.86
	KNN	91.5	18.6	85.1	0.86
	NB	88.9	41.8	44.2	0.78
	RF	93.6	48.5	79.4	0.92
	XGB	93.7	51.6	78.2	0.92
	RNN	92.8	39.6	77.9	0.87

NOTE: Gray cells denote performance of at least 10 percent below the maximum value for that metric.

19

XGB are in the same family of methods and performed very similarly overall. For brevity, we will focus the remainder of this chapter on the performance characteristics of XGB, which is our preferred model.

The 3Y Ave assigns the same separation probability to all individuals within a given AFSC and YOS. Even within an AFSC and YOS, however, separation rates may vary widely by individual. Because the 3Y Ave captures only group-level effects, it does not distinguish between individuals who are more or less likely to separate. This is why the individual-level performance of the 3Y Ave is so low, as compared with the performance of other methods.

To illustrate, Figure 4.2. shows attributes and predicted separation probabilities for officers in the pilot (i.e., AFSC 11X) inventory with 12 YOS. The 3Y Ave assigns the same separation probability to all individuals (25.2 percent). XGB takes individual attributes into account, and so it assigns vastly higher separation probabilities to the officers with a projected date of separation on record (98.3 versus 15.2 percent). Of the officers without a separation date on record, XGB assigns a higher separation probability to those who are separation eligible (37.8 versus 4.1 percent). Finally, regardless of whether or not an officer is separation eligible, XGB assigns higher separation probabilities to those who are still at the rank of O-3 after 12 YOS. This example is merely illustrative. The decision trees that XGB learns are actually much more complex, and by grouping officers using additional variables besides AFSC and YOS, XGB greatly improves individual-level predictions.

Figure 4.2. Separation Rates for Pilots with 12 Years of Service

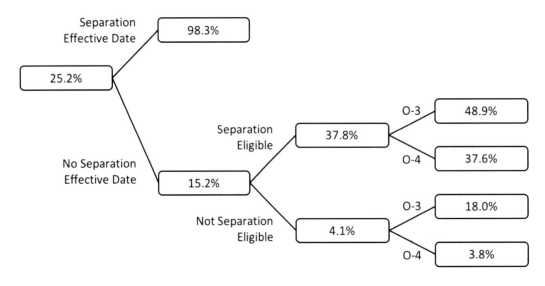

An underlying assumption in how we operationalized these models is that improving individual-level predictions will also improve estimates of group-level separation rates. To confirm that this was true, we averaged retention outcomes and model predictions across individuals by AFSC and YOS. Across all combinations of AFSC and YOS, XGB predictions were within 0.9 percent and 1.0 percent of the observed separation rates for officers and enlisted personnel on average, whereas predictions based on the 3Y Ave were within 1.4 percent and 1.6 percent of observed separation rates. In other words, improving individual-level predictions by using XGB did reduce error in estimates of group-level separation rates.

Predicting Separations in Future Years

In addition to predicting separations for the upcoming year, it would be useful to predict whether an individual will remain in the force across longer time horizons—for example, from two years to five years into the future. To do so, we retrained the XGB models to predict whether an individual would separate within the next two, three, four, or five years. We generated corresponding yearly predictions for the 3Y Ave by multiplying the annual separation probabilities within YOS and AFSC. For these exercises, the test year remained the same, but the window of time covered in the training data had to be moved back to accommodate the longer time horizon.

Figure 4.3. shows model accuracy for the 3Y Ave and XGB model by the length of the prediction interval. Performance for both methods decreases with the length of the prediction interval. This is partly because fewer individuals separate over a one-year period, and so the

Figure 4.3. Model Accuracy for Predicting Separations with Multi-Year Horizons

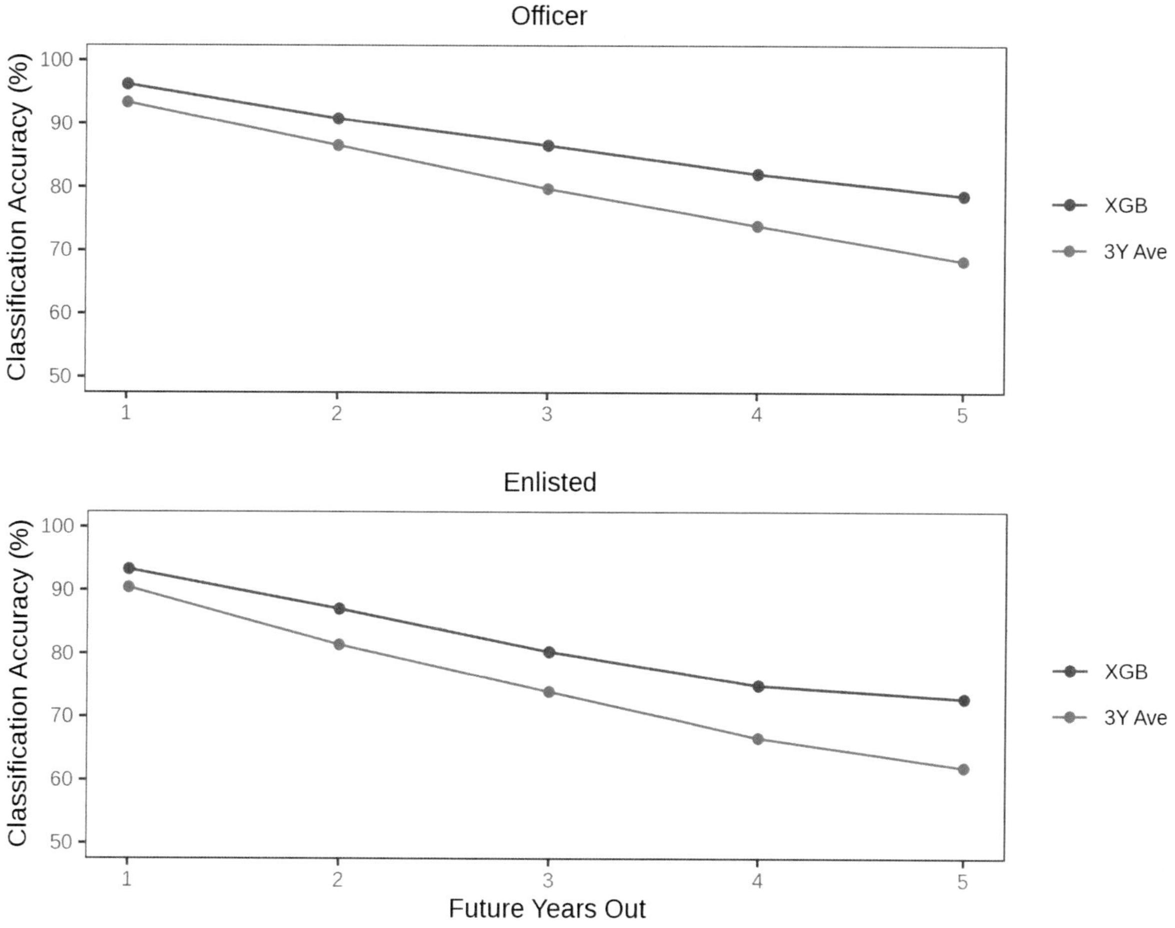

prediction task is more difficult over longer intervals. This is also because certain variables that signal separation appear in personnel files only shortly before a servicemember separates. Even so, XGB did a reasonably good job of predicting separations over the complete five-year horizon.

Variable Importance and Relationship to Conceptual Framework

As mentioned earlier, with ML there is a trade-off between flexibility and interpretability—and there can also be a trade-off between accuracy and interpretability. The ease with which data can be included in an ML model and the accuracy of the model are strengths; however, policymakers are also interested in which variables are most predictive of a retention decision.

To determine variable importance in the XGB models, we decomposed the decision trees and calculated the relative gain in predictive accuracy attributed to each variable.[7] Table 4.2. shows the 20 variables with highest gain in the officer and enlisted models. In terms of the variables' origins, most came from MilPDS and are readily available for Air Force HR functions. In terms of the conceptual framework for personnel retention, variables came primarily from collective characteristics, and also from HR systems and practices and environmental characteristics.

Table 4.2. Variable Importance in Officer and Enlisted Models

Variable	Source	Category	Officer Gain (Percentage)	Enlisted Gain (Percentage)
Separation effective date listed	MilPDS	Collective characteristics	36.6	13.5
Reenlistment eligibility status	MilPDS	Collective characteristics	—	17.7
Max. ADSC time remaining	MilPDS	Collective characteristics	9.1	3.0
Separation eligible	MilPDS	Collective characteristics	5.0	5.7
3Y Ave sep. rate by AFSC and YOS	MilPDS	Collective characteristics	3.9	4.5
Max. enlistment term time remaining	MilPDS	Collective characteristics	—	4.2
3Y Ave sep. rate by AFSC and YOS among separation eligible individuals	MilPDS	Collective characteristics	2.3	1.8
YOS	MilPDS	Collective characteristics	2.2	1.5
Age	MilPDS	Collective characteristics	2.5	—
Duty AFSC	MilPDS	HR systems and practices	1.8	1.6
Location	MilPDS	Collective characteristics	1.7	1.5
Reenlistment eligibility status group	MilPDS	Collective characteristics	—	3.2
Enlisted performance report ratings	MilPDS	Collective characteristics	—	3.2
Previous year separation rate among AFSC age-group cohort	MilPDS	Collective characteristics	1.6	1.5

---

[7] Each split in the decision tree is based on one variable. Gain is calculated as the relative improvement in prediction accuracy resulting from all splits involving a given variable.

Variable	Source	Category	Officer Gain (Percentage)	Enlisted Gain (Percentage)
Rank	MilPDS	Collective characteristics	1.7	1.4
Nondeployable—retainability[b]	MilPDS	Collective characteristics	2.1	—
Nondeployable—physical	MilPDS	Collective characteristics	1.4	1.5
Career field manning	MilPDS	Collective characteristics	1.7	1.2
BMI	AFFMS	Collective characteristics	1.4	1.5
Aerobic fitness test performance	AFFMS	Collective characteristics	1.3	1.5
Local median compensation	MilPDS and American Community Survey (ACS)	Environmental characteristics	1.3	1.2
Core ID (officer) or control AFSC (enlisted)	MilPDS	HR systems and practices	—	1.3
Promotion status[a]	MilPDS	HR systems and practices	2.2	—
Percentage core ID or control AFSC that is female	MilPDS	Collective characteristics	1.1	—
Medal count	MilPDS	HR systems and practices	1.2	—

NOTES: The table omits percentages if the variable did not fall in the top 20 for both officer and enlisted models.
[a] Promotion status indicates whether an officer has been considered/selected for promotion to the next grade and for which zones.
[b] Retainability affects officer and enlisted capacity to deploy in cases where members have a date of separation that would prevent them from completing the required deployment duration.

The full models included dozens of variables, yet the analysis of variable importance suggests that models with far fewer variables may achieve similar levels of performance. This would be attractive in terms of increasing the interpretability of the models and decreasing the logistical challenges of gathering and maintaining the variables needed for them. Specifically, many of the most important variables involve information about service commitments that is easily accessible to Air Force analysts. This finding suggests that folding this information into existing practices would be a low-cost "quick win" for the Air Force. More broadly, this finding highlights an advantage that the Air Force has over civilian employers, which is that the personnel system naturally generates precise indicators of the likelihood of imminent separation.

To evaluate the suitability of reduced models, we retained the ten most important variables from the full officer and enlisted models in addition to AFSC and YOS (Table 4.2). We then trained and tested XGB with the simplified variable sets. Table 4.3 compares the performance of the full and simplified models. Remarkably, the performance of the simplified models was only slightly less than the performance of the full models when predicting outcomes for the next year (Table 4.3, 1 Year Out), and only moderately less when predicting outcomes for the next five years (Table 4.3, 5 Years Out).

Table 4.3. Results for One-Year and Five-Year Predictions Using Full and Simplified Extreme Gradient Boosting Model

| Sample | Method | 1 Year Out | | | | 5 Years Out |
		Accuracy	Recall (Percentage)	Precision (Percentage)	AUC	Accuracy (Percentage)
Officer	Full XGB	96.1	52.0	90.1	0.94	78.7
	Simplified XGB	96.0	50.4	89.5	0.92	75.6
Enlisted	Full XGB	93.7	51.6	78.2	0.92	70.6
	Simplified XGB	93.4	47.0	78.0	0.91	68.1

Summary

The Air Force currently uses three-year moving averages by AFSC and YOS to forecast separations. The results of our analyses showed that modern ML algorithms such as XGB can increase the accuracy of individual-level predictions and that these improvements result in more accurate group-level estimates for separation rates. The full models used dozens of variables from multiple sources, yet far simpler models that used ten variables that are already available to the Air Force also performed extremely well. This suggests that it would be beneficial and feasible to use ML to forecast officer and enlisted separations.

5. How Retention Predictions Can Be Used to Generate Warnings

Having achieved an accurate model that uses available data to predict future retention, the final step in the data-mining process is to apply the information from the model to improve decisionmaking. Certain HR processes can use retention predictions directly as an input, but one of the design specifications of REWS was a capability that could scan across subpopulations and alert HR managers to areas at risk of a future retention problem.

To meet this need, we created a prototype application based on predictions from the top-performing ML model in the previous chapter, which guides users through a process of generating warnings, investigating those warnings, and deciding on a policy response. Figure 5.1 outlines the workflow that informs the basic structure of the application, and each box represents a panel or page with which the user can interact. The following paragraphs discuss the intent and functionality of each step (with appendices containing further methodological details), along with illustrations of the functionality through a "worked example."

Figure 5.1. Decision Workflow for Retention Early Warning System Application

  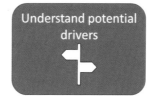 

Managers across the Air Force's HR organizations focus on different aspects of the workforce, so potential users require the flexibility to aggregate predictions across various categories of personnel. The first step in the workflow is to select the population categories of interest. For example, users in AF/A1P dealing with promotions might view retention predictions by grade and development category; AF/A1X users concerned with career field sustainment planning could view predictions by career field; and AF/A1D users could view predictions by demographic group or according to education credentials.

Figure 5.2 shows the Introduction landing page of the REWS application and illustrates the first step of the workflow by selecting a set of population categories. This example assumes the perspective of a functional manager concerned with enlisted intelligence specialties, so the sidebar panel of the figure shows the manager setting the global filter to the core specialties of 1N0 through 1N4.

The Early Warning page of the application will then display the predictions, as both rates and expected numbers of personnel, for each group that the user has selected. The user can then both

Figure 5.2. Using the Global Filter to Select Population Categories

select a time horizon and warning thresholds for either the rates or the personnel numbers and disaggregate the warnings to further explore subgroups within the selected populations. This page offers the following two options for generating warnings:[1]

- *Retention-based warning.* This warning will highlight categories of personnel in which predicted losses deviate from what a planner would expect based on recent retention patterns. It compares the model predictions with a three-year moving average by career field and YOS.
- *Inventory-based warning.* This warning will highlight categories of personnel in which model predictions imply that the inventory will grow or shrink over the selected time horizon. It converts the model predictions into a rough projection of the future inventory and compares this level with the initial inventory.[2]

The retention-based warning is useful in cases where planning assumptions presume that retention will be stable, because it will flag areas where those planning assumptions could fail in the short term. For example, planners in AF/A1 set accession targets so that they can replace

---

[1] We considered a warning based on the gap between predicted retention and authorizations, but abandoned this idea for two reasons. First, the authorization codes are generally less specific than the personnel categories that many HR managers are interested in. Second, an authorization-based warning would highlight chronic shortages or structural flaws in the authorization structure, which does not align with the functionality that HR managers desire for this capability.

[2] To detect inventory deviations, we created a simple inventory model. The model took as a starting point the existing size of the inventory. Based on five years' historical data, we computed the average annual inflow to that inventory, and the average outflow for nonseparation reasons. Using the ML predictions, we then determined the expected outflow due to separations. The projected size of the future inventory equaled its existing size, plus expected inflow, minus total expected outflow.

long-run losses in each career field. The retention-based warning forms a useful check on these assumptions, because it will highlight career fields where near-term losses are likely to deviate from the long-run averages; planners will thus be able to consider the consequences of these deviations and potentially adjust planned targets to mitigate them.

A drawback of the retention-based warning is that it tends to flag any population category that differs systematically from the population average. For instance, if a user were to select separation eligibility as a population category, there would always be a warning because separation-eligible members have above-average separation risk. The inventory-based warning is immune to this flaw, because it considers possible changes only in the inventory in each category and does not involve a comparison of model predictions with any "expected" level of retention. The inventory-based warning is most useful in cases where planners seek to maintain or increase the number of personnel with a particular characteristic, but they lack clear expectations for normal levels of retention.

Figure 5.3 continues the example by showing the retention-based warnings for all enlisted intelligence specialties, as well as the same warning display when the user disaggregates the predictions by three-digit core specialty. The default user-specified thresholds will trigger warnings when the model's predictions deviate from the moving averages by at least

Figure 5.3. Retention-Based Warnings for Intelligence Specialties

All intelligence specialties

Choose whether the table shows warnings based on predicted losses or predicted inventories.
◉ Model Table❶ ○ Inventory Table❶

Inventory Size	Predicted Separation Rate: 3Y Ave	Predicted Separation Rate: ML Model	Difference in Predicted Separation Rates	Difference in Predicted Number of Separations
All	All	All	All	All
14,854	9.8%	12.4%	2.5%	377

Disaggregated by specialty

Core AFSC	Inventory Size	Predicted Separation Rate: 3Y Ave	Predicted Separation Rate: ML Model	Difference in Predicted Separation Rates	Difference in Predicted Number of Separations
All	All	All	All	All	All
1N0	3,269	10.3%	11.7%	1.4%	46
1N4	3,008	7.0%	9.7%	2.7%	80
1N1	3,013	10.2%	12.8%	2.7%	80
1N2	2,142	9.3%	12.0%	2.7%	59
1N3	3,422	11.9%	15.2%	3.3%	113

two percentage points *and* when this difference results in a deviation in separations of at least 20 personnel. The top panel shows that predicted losses for all intelligence personnel are 2.5 percentage points higher than one would expect based on the recent patterns in the moving average. This deviation is most extreme for the 1N3 career field (cryptologic language analyst), but falls short of the warning threshold for the 1N0 career field (operations intelligence). Figure 5.3 does not display the inventory-based warning, but if the user were to click the radio button at the top (selecting "Inventory Table" rather than "Model Table"), he or she would find that these predictions, combined with recent inflows, suggest that there will be a decline in the personnel inventory for these specialties.

Figure 5.4 presents another example from the Early Warning page: the inventory-based warnings for officers whose core specialty is developmental engineering (62X). These warnings use the same thresholds as before, but they are now based on a comparison of the current inventory to the projected inventory. The top panel shows that REWS predicts that the inventory will decline slightly, but not enough to trigger a warning under the current settings. However, when the user disaggregates the predictions by education level, the results show a mix of potentially important human capital gains and losses. Predicted losses among officers with master's degrees and doctorates are disproportionately high, but partially offset by gains among officers holding only a bachelor's degree.

Figure 5.4. Inventory-Based Warnings for Developmental Engineering Officer Specialties

All developmental engineers

Inventory Size	Projected Inventory Size	Percentage Change in Inventory Size	Change in Inventory Size
All	All	All	All
3,384	3,318	-2.0%	-66

Disaggregated by educational attainment

Education Level	Inventory Size	Projected Inventory Size	Percentage Change in Inventory Size	Change in Inventory Size
All	All	All	All	All
DOCTORATE	220	206	-6.4%	-14
AWARDED MASTERS DEGREE	1,999	1,889	-5.5%	-110
GRADUATE WORK - NO DEGREE	33	32	-3.0%	-1
AWARDED BACCALAUREATE DEGREE	1,119	1,178	5.3%	59

The next step in the warning workflow aims to help the user understand the factors that underlie the shift in expected retention. The Decomposition page allows the user to explore whether population shifts in underlying characteristics are driving the differences between the model predictions and recent history. For example, if a wave of retirements were approaching, the ML model would project an increase in separations because characteristics such as age, YOS, and separation eligibility would shift. The decomposition page would then provide insight into the warning by highlighting these characteristics as important contributors to the warning.

Figure 5.5 shows the Decomposition page for the example of enlisted intelligence specialties. In the example, the user has selected separation eligibility, marital status, rank, and years of service as potential explanatory factors of interest. The length of the bars in the table show the magnitude of the impact of each characteristic, while the color denotes whether the characteristic contributes to the warning or whether it is a mitigating factor. The result informs the user that the shifts in the proportion of members in the E-6 pay grade, the proportion that are separation

Figure 5.5. Potential Drivers of the Warning for Intelligence Specialties

Decomposition page: which factors are driving the warnings?

Select the population that generated the warning you are interested in and find out which factors strongly contribute to the predicted warning.
2.79 percentage points is the difference in overall separation rate between the model (12.37%) and the moving average (9.59%).

0% of this difference is explained by population shift with respect to the selected covariates.

Yellow variables contribute to the difference between model predictions and recent losses.
Blue variables are mitigating factors that might be changing, but in a way that tends to reduce the difference between model predictions and recent losses. In other words, the specific warning would be even larger if not for the influence of Blue variables.

Show 10 ˅ entries   Search: [   ]

Decomposition Covariates

yos

rankE6

rankE7

rankE3

sep.eligible0Yes

rankE4

maritalSINGLE

rankE5

rankE2

maritalSEPARATED

Showing 1 to 10 of 13 entries   Previous 1 2 Next

29

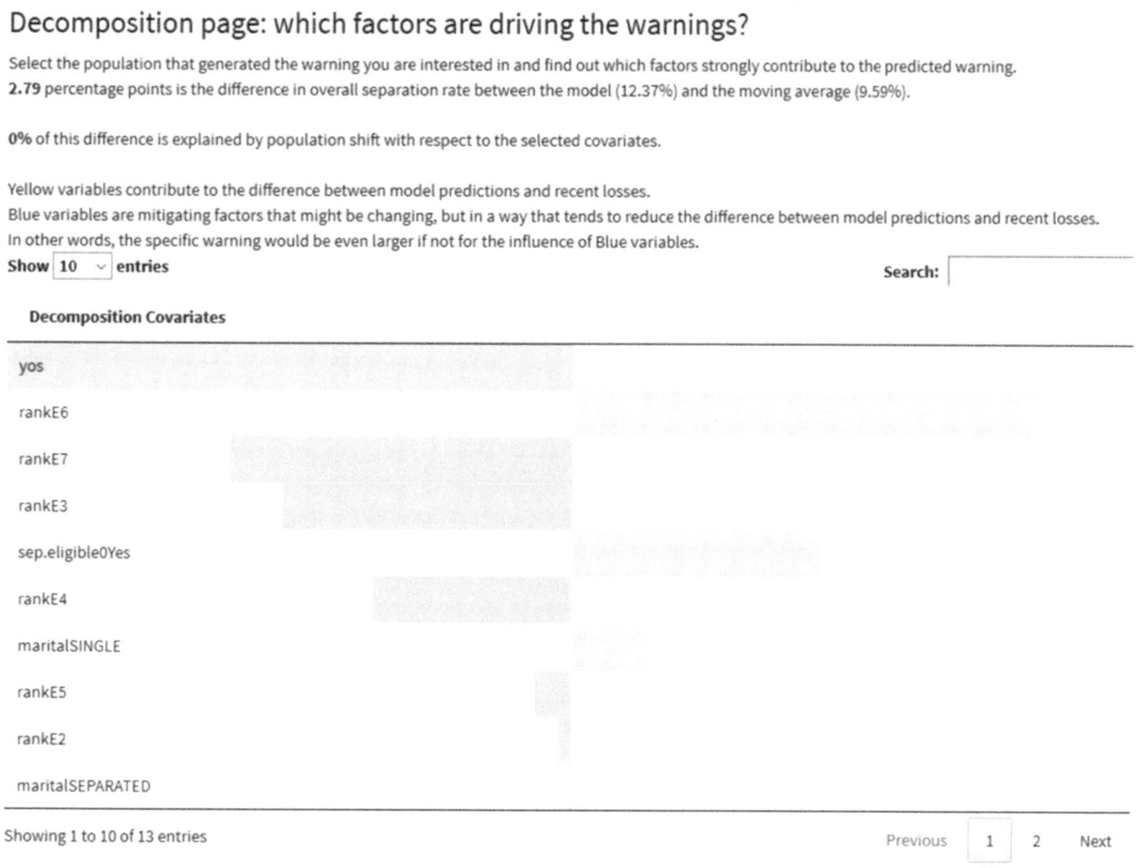

eligible, and the proportion that are single potentially contribute to higher-than-expected losses in the coming year.[3]

The Policy Impact page allows the user to explore the scope for addressing warnings through policy. This page presents the predicted number of personnel remaining by YOS, along with the number expected to separate voluntarily, which acts as an upper boundary for potential policy improvements. Users can then apply policy effects from the research literature to the separation-eligible population and observe the improvements in the number of additional personnel who would remain in the workforce (see Appendix E for the methodology that the application uses to apply the policy effects to the predictions).

Figure 5.6 shows the Policy Impact display for the worked example of enlisted intelligence specialties.

Figure 5.6. Policy Impact Page for Intelligence Specialties

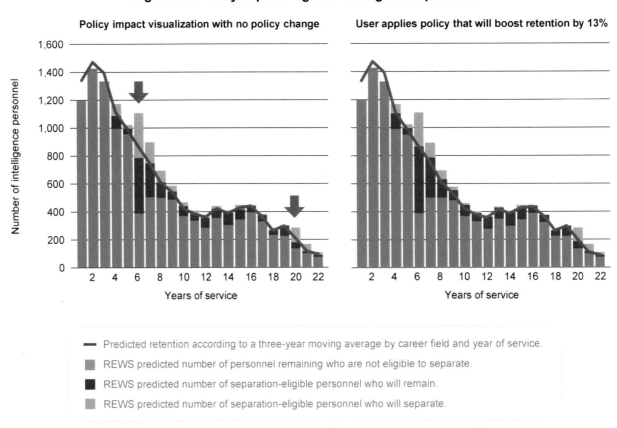

---

[3] In its current form, the tool does not provide feedback on whether the shift that contributes to the warning is positive or negative. A shift in either direction could contribute to warnings or mitigate them. For example, if the model predicts higher losses than the moving average, an increase in a variable that is positively associated with losses would contribute to the warning. If the model had predicted lower losses than the moving average, the same shift would have tended to mitigate the warning.

30

The left panel of the figure includes two red arrows highlighting the sixth and twentieth year of service, because these particular areas feature the largest gaps between the moving average (red line) and ML model's predictions (height of the purple bar). Thus, predictions in these years are the primary drivers of the original warning. From this point, the hypothetical manager can apply a policy effect, the impact of which is estimated from prior research (some examples of which are provided in the application itself), and observe the impact. Alternatively, the user can use the policy effect slider to find out how effective a policy would need to be in order to remove the warning, which is shown in the panel on the right hand side. A 13-percentage-point increase in retention likelihood among those eligible to separate would close the gap between the moving average and the model predictions. An effect of this magnitude would be large relative to the example policy effects from the research literature. For instance, prior research has shown that an increase in the SRB multiplier is associated with less than a 1-percentage-point boost to retention overall (Joffrion and Wozny, 2015).

The final page in the REWS application, Download, allows Air Force analysts to download model predictions and inventory projections for any set of population categories (by career field and YOS, for instance) for further analysis or inclusion into other models. This capability, in addition to the workflow in the application, allows a wide variety of potential users to access and browse the REWS outputs and apply their results to decisionmaking.

6. Next Steps for Further Development and Implementation

This report documents our approach to design an REWS capability to assist HR decisionmaking, drawing on the emerging workflows and methods from applied data science. Nearly all data-mining processes and workflows depict projects in a circular fashion, which indicates that the initial capability ought to be subject to a process of continued feedback and refinement. Thus, we conclude the report with next steps for HR managers to consider regarding further development and implementation of the REWS concepts and decision-support tool.

Feedback from Human Resources Managers Should Guide Decisionmaking Refinements

Our review of prior research shows that a large body of work exists for understanding and predicting retention decisions. There is much less information to draw on regarding how practitioners should use retention predictions to make better management decisions. This initial version of REWS incorporates decisionmaking functionality that we developed through conversations with potential users, but the best course for further improvements of this aspect of the REWS application is to make the application widely available and collect feedback from users on gaps between the application's functionality and their decision needs.

Improvements to Survey Data Collection Could Enhance the Retention Early Warning System's Ability to Anticipate Retention Trends

Member perceptions and attitudes are the most promising source of information that is currently unavailable to REWS. While we were not able to analyze data from the Air Force's retention and climate surveys, the infrequency of these surveys makes them unlikely to significantly improve the models over the existing information. As we discuss in Chapter 3, adjustments to retention survey implementation could provide better inputs to future versions of REWS, and the Air Force could design these adjustments in a way that is cost-neutral with respect to the burden on respondents.

Simplified Data Inputs Offer a Simpler Way to Refresh Predictions

Guided by our framework from the extensive literature on employee turnover, we included a broad array of potential sources of information in REWS. However, our analysis revealed that it is possible to generate predictions that perform similarly well with a limited set of features and are easily accessible to Air Force analysts. Thus, future efforts to refresh and update REWS could begin by examining the performance of a limited set of readily available data inputs, compared with the benchmarks provided in this report. Then, analysts could consider broadening the inputs based on whether they improve the performance of the system over the base set of easy-to-collect data inputs.

View This Effort as a Down Payment for a Longer Term, Continually Improving Business Intelligence Capability

While the previous chapters summarize our research methods and results, the full set of project deliverables includes the REWS decision-support tool, its associated components, and the input files and codes that define the data pipeline. In addition to making more tactical improvements to the usability of the initial version, the Air Force analytic community could target strategic efforts toward refining the data inputs and processing, improving on the current REWS ML models, and expanding the coverage to new populations, such as the civilian workforce or the reserve components. As Air Force HR managers work to improve their data architecture and adopt decision-support tools such as REWS, they will no doubt encounter challenges (see Appendix E for a brief discussion of the most relevant challenges to REWS). Like the Joint Operations doctrine that Air Force decisionmakers are familiar with, data-mining process models presume that this will be the case. In response, they prescribe a medicine of continuous assessment and refinement to ensure the overall effort progresses toward the organization's objectives.

Appendix A. Creating the Analytic Data File

To create an analytical file for analyzing and predicting servicemember retention, we gathered monthly extracts from MilPDS. These gave individual month records for all officers and enlisted personnel in the active component from FY 2005 to FY 2019. We collapsed across months to create analytical files with annual timesteps. We added annual physical fitness test outcomes gathered from AFFMS over the same date range. These outcomes included scores and exemptions from the four subcomponents of the Air Force fitness test: aerobic, push-ups, sit-ups, and abdominal circumference (U.S. Air Force, 2015). All scores were normalized by servicemember age group and gender. Fitness outcomes also included whether the servicemember was exempt from the full test (i.e., composite exemption) and the servicemember's BMI. Additionally, we added deployment dates gathered from DCAPES. Finally, we added enlisted promotion data including enlisted performance reports ratings, skills knowledge test scores, and promotion fitness examination scores. The latter two were normalized by version and promotion cycle.

To define labor market characteristics, we used U.S. Census ACS data and the Current Population Survey (CPS). To determine local labor market characteristics, we reweighted economic indicators reported at the county level to create commuting-zone-level median values. We then assigned local labor market variables (median household income, unemployment, and relative income) to servicemembers based on their current commuting zone. To determine occupational labor market characteristics, we mapped military occupational classification (MOC) codes to standard occupational classification (SOC) codes using a DMDC crosswalk. We then assigned occupational economic indicators to individuals based on their MOC (relative income, unemployment). For MOCs without matching SOCs, we used national averages of high school graduates to derive values for enlisted personnel, and national averages of college graduates to derive values for officers. To determine relative income, we took regular military compensation values from compensation greenbooks.

Appendix B. Machine Learning Algorithms

To model servicemember retention decisions, we tested six traditional and contemporary ML approaches to classification. The approaches include

- **General Linear Model (GLM).** GLM treats the outcome as the weighted sum of the values of predictor variables. GLM estimates the set of weights (or coefficients) to apply to predictor variables to increase the accuracy of predicted outcomes.
- **K-Nearest Neighbors (KNN).** KNN stores all training cases. When a new case is encountered, it is classified based on the plurality vote of the k training cases that are most similar to it (i.e., the k-nearest neighbors).
- **Naïve Bayes (NB).** NB uses Bayes's theorem to estimate the probability of the outcome separately for each variable. Based on the naïve assumption that the variables are independent, NB combines probability estimates across all variables to classify new cases.
- **Random Forests (RF).** RF learns decision trees, which are sequences of yes/no decision rules used to classify new cases. RF learns multiple such trees using different subsets of predictor variables, and then averages predictions across the ensemble of trees.
- **Extreme Gradient Boosting (XGB).** Like RF, XGB models also learn an ensemble of decision trees, but in a sequential fashion. Each tree in the sequence reduces the residual classification error that remains after applying all of the earlier trees.
- **Recurrent Neural Network (RNN).** RNN architecture contains units arranged into an input layer, hidden layers, and an output layer. The units are connected, and the weights of the connections between units are learned during training. When an input variable is provided to the RNN, activation passes from the input layer, through the hidden layer(s), to the output layer, and is shaped by the connection weights.

These classification algorithms vary in terms of flexibility (see Table B.1). Generally, methods that are more flexible also make more accurate predictions (given enough training data), but this is ultimately an empirical question. Thus, we implemented all of the methods listed in Table B.1 to assess their ability to predict officer and enlisted separations. These algorithms also vary in terms of interpretability. This is less straightforward to measure, and the importance of interpretability may depend on how the classification outcomes are to be used.

Table B.1. Description and Characteristics of Classification Algorithms

Method	Flexibility	Interpretability
GLM	Low	High
KNN	Low	Medium
NB	Low	High
RF	High	Medium
XGB	High	Low
RNN	High	Low

All ML algorithms were implemented, trained, and evaluated using the R computing language. Table B.2 lists the ML approaches along with the R packages used to implement them. Some of the approaches include meta-parameters, which are high-level parameters that control how the approach is implemented, as in, for example, the number of neighbors to include in the plurality vote in KNN. Table B.2 lists the meta-parameters that were estimated for each approach. All other meta-parameters were set to default values.

Table B.2. Machine Learning Algorithms Used

Method	Package	Meta-Parameters
GLM	glm (base R)	None
KNN	fastKNN	Neighborhood size
RF	ranger	Number of variable per tree (mtry) Number of trees (num.trees)
NB	naivebayes	Laplace smoothing (laplace) Density estimate for metric predictors (usekernel)
XGB	xgboost	Learning rate (eta) Max tree depth (max_depth) Number of rounds (nrounds)
RNN	keras	Batch size (batch_size) Validation split (validation_split)

We trained the methods using ten consecutive years of historical data and then tested the predictions during the following, out-of-sample year. Given the large number of individual-year records contained in the ten-year training sets, we sampled 50 percent of officer records and 25 percent of enlisted records. Model meta-parameters were tuned using fivefold cross-validation over subsets of the training data.

Both RFXGB can naturally capture interactions via the tree structures they learn. Likewise, RNN can naturally capture interactions via the connection weights between units and the nonlinear activation functions they use. This is a major advantage of these approaches—the vast number of potential two-way and higher-dimensional interactions do not need to be explicitly specified. The remaining methods (GLM, KNN, and NB) do not capture interactions by default. Because we expected the effects of many variables to be modulated by AFSC, we fitted the latter group of methods (GLM, KNN, and NB) separately to each AFSC. We fitted the former pair of methods (RF and XGB) across all AFSCs because they are able to capture interactions between AFSC and other variables.

The RNN that we used contained gated recurrent units, which allow it to learn from sequential dependencies between servicemember variables across multiple years. The RNN also used embedding layers to reduce high-dimensional categorical variables to lower-dimensional continuous variables.

Some categorical variables had an extremely high number of levels (e.g., location, education level, and duty status). To retain these variables for all methods besides the RNN, we used an approach called *impact coding.*[1] This is a bridge from NB where categorical variable levels are replaced by the relative frequency of the target (i.e., separation) associated with each in the training data. In this case, we replaced categorical variable levels with the *change* in the frequency of separation associated with each. For example, Figure B.1 shows the

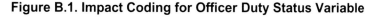

Figure B.1. Impact Coding for Officer Duty Status Variable

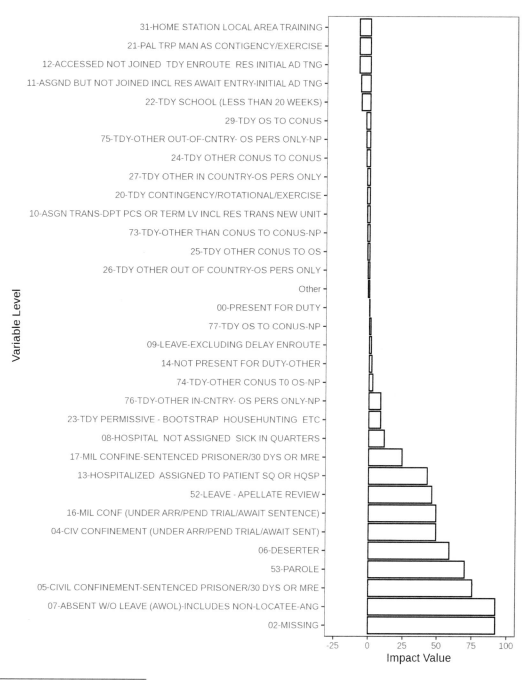

_____

[1] The RNN used embedding layers to reduce the high-dimensional categorical variables to lower-dimensional continuous values.

mapping from categorical levels of the duty status variable to continuous values that represent the change in frequency of separation for officers. Positive values indicate an increased probability of separation. These continuous values were used in place of categorical levels by the ML algorithms.

Appendix C. Decomposition Methodology

One way to interpret the output of a "black-box" model is to train a more decipherable "student" or "mimic" model—for which inference techniques have already been developed—on the model output. This is distinct from training a mimic model on the true labels. Take as an example a linear regression mimic model. High-order interaction effects or nonlinear relationships are captured by the black-box model and reflected in the estimates. Then, regressing the estimates on the original data matrix relates the information learned by the black-box model to the feature set.

Interpreting the departure of the model estimates from expectation—in the context of Air Force inventory forecasting, expectation is the historical trend line—is a subtly different question. The policymaker is concerned with the difference between the model's individual-level prediction and the separation rate for the individual's AFSC-YOS cohort averaged over the previous three years. It may be simultaneously true that (1) the population shifts year over year, which contributes to altered separation rates, and (2) the model detects signals that the moving average calculation misses. By way of the Blinder-Oaxaca Decomposition (Blinder, 1973; Oaxaca, 1973), mimic models can be used to partition the difference between model estimates and the historical trend line. The Blinder-Oaxaca Decomposition is a traditional method in economics that here decomposes difference into (1) that which can be explained by population shift and (2) that which cannot be explained by population shift.

Let A refer to the model and B refer to the moving average. Suppose there are n individuals in the held-out testing set. Then, $\widehat{Y_A}$ is the $n \times 1$ vector that gives model estimates for the year under consideration. $\widehat{Y_B}$ is the $n \times 1$ vector that gives the separation rate averaged over the previous three years, broken out by individuals' AFSC and YOS.

In both cases, $\hat{Y} \in [0, 1]$ is the expected probability of separation and not the true separation outcome $Y \in \{0, 1\}$. Let $\overline{Y_A}$ and $\overline{Y_B}$ denote the average over all n estimates for the respective methods. Then, $\Delta\overline{Y} = \overline{Y_A} - \overline{Y_B}$ is the difference in mean predicted separation rate between the model estimates and the moving average estimates. If $\Delta\overline{Y} > 0$, the model predicts a separation rate greater than the historical trend line, and retention will be lower than expected.

Let X_A represent the $n \times p$ matrix giving observed values for p covariates. $\overline{X_A}$ is the $p \times 1$ vector giving the average over the n individuals for each covariate. For example, the jth element of $\overline{X_A}$ is given by $\overline{X_{A_j}} = \frac{1}{n}\sum_{i=1}^{n} X_{A_{ij}}$.

X_B is also an $n \times p$ matrix, but element ij is the average value of covariate j observed in the ith individual's AFSC-YOS cohort over the past three years. Consider sit-up performance for an officer in AFSC 44X with ten years of service. In X_A, this officer's sit-up performance is the true number of sit-ups he was able to do in the test set year. In X_B, this officer's sit-up performance is the mean number of sit-ups achieved in a single test by one officer in AFSC 44X with ten years of service, averaged over the three years previous to the test set year. $\overline{X_B}$ is the $p \times 1$ vector giving the mean of these moving average covariate values across all n individuals.

The overall difference $\Delta \bar{Y}$ can be decomposed:

$$\Delta \bar{Y} = (\overline{X_A} - \overline{X_B})^T \widehat{\beta_R} + \overline{X_A}^T (\widehat{\beta_A} - \widehat{\beta_R}) + \overline{X_B}^T (\widehat{\beta_R} - \widehat{\beta_B}).$$

$\widehat{\beta_R}$ is the reference coefficient that arises from the linear regression of $\begin{bmatrix} \widehat{Y_A} \\ \widehat{Y_B} \end{bmatrix}$ on $\begin{bmatrix} X_A \\ X_B \end{bmatrix}$. $\widehat{\beta_A}$ and $\widehat{\beta_B}$ are from the regression of $\widehat{Y_A}$ on X_A and the regression of $\widehat{Y_B}$ on X_B, respectively. $(\overline{X_A} - \overline{X_B})^T \widehat{\beta_R}$ is the portion of $\Delta \bar{Y}$ that is explained by a change in demographics from the previous three years to the testing year. $\frac{(\overline{X_A} - \overline{X_B})^T \widehat{\beta_R}}{\Delta \bar{Y}}$ is the proportion of the difference that can be explained by population shift. The latter two summands in $\Delta \bar{Y}$ are the unexplained portion of $\Delta \bar{Y}$ and, loosely, are the consequence of the inherent difference in technique between the two methods. $(\overline{X_A} - \overline{X_B})^T \widehat{\beta_R}$ can be further broken down:

$$(\overline{X_A} - \overline{X_B})^T \widehat{\beta_R} = (\overline{X_{A_1}} - \overline{X_{B_1}})^T \widehat{\beta_{R_1}} + (\overline{X_{A_2}} - \overline{X_{B_2}})^T \widehat{\beta_{R_2}} + \cdots,$$

where $\overline{X_{A_1}}$ is the mean value of the first covariate in X_A, $\overline{X_{B_1}}$ is the mean value of the first covariate in X_B, and $\widehat{\beta_{R_1}}$ is the first element of $\widehat{\beta_R}$. $(\overline{X_{A_1}} - \overline{X_{B_1}})^T \widehat{\beta_{R_1}}$ is the contribution of the shift in demographics to the difference $\Delta \bar{Y}$ with respect to the first covariate.

Consider $(\overline{X_{A_k}} - \overline{X_{B_k}})^T \widehat{\beta_{R_k}}$. If the signs of $(\overline{X_{A_k}} - \overline{X_{B_k}})^T \widehat{\beta_{R_k}}$ and $\Delta \bar{Y}$ agree—i.e., $(\overline{X_{A_k}} - \overline{X_{B_k}})^T \widehat{\beta_{R_k}} > 0$ and $\Delta \bar{Y} > 0$ or $(\overline{X_{A_k}} - \overline{X_{B_k}})^T \widehat{\beta_{R_k}} < 0$ and $\Delta \bar{Y} < 0$—then population shift with respect to the kth covariate drives the model estimates' departure from the historical trend. If the signs of $(\overline{X_{A_k}} - \overline{X_{B_k}})^T \widehat{\beta_{R_k}}$ and $\Delta \bar{Y}$ disagree, then population shift with respect to the kth covariate mitigates the departure. Population shift may have occurred with respect to the kth covariate, but in a way that tends to reduce the difference between model estimates and the moving average estimates. In other words, the specific warning would be even larger if not for the influence of the kth covariate.

When we operationalized this in the REWS application, we left it up to the user to select covariates for X. This does not need to be the full set of features used in the model, and might be motivated by the policymaker's substantive knowledge of manpower and personnel in the Air Force.

Appendix D. Literature Review Methodology

The purpose of the literature review was twofold. First, we used the literature to identify potential antecedents of turnover across a variety of sources and settings, including the private sector. Second, we used existing literature to develop a model for thinking conceptually about the causes of turnover and determining which data sources we incorporated into the model.

We pulled articles from the following databases: Government Accountability Office, Defense Technical Information Center, Psych Info, Web of Sci, Business Source Complete, Business Book Summary, eBook Business Collection, and Policy File Index. These articles included government and academic documents; some of these documents were specific to the military, while many were academic studies, which focused mainly on the private sector. The academic documents were primarily from psychology and business. We used a Boolean search strategy using synonyms for retention. For example, we searched for the following terms: *retention*, *turnover*, *quit*, *layoff*, *resignation*, *exit survey*, *exit interview*, *attrition*, *career continuance*, *resignation*, and *termination*. To limit the studies to a work or organizational context, we also included the following related words: *employment* or *employer*, *work*, *organization*, and *job*. We limited our search to only those studies published after 2005 and English-language publications. We combined all publications in EndNote, a document management software, and removed all duplicates.

After downloading all literature, we first noted any meaningful or consistent definitions used in the field and seminal models of turnover and retention. Second, we coded all potential antecedents of turnover or retention. We entered each antecedent in a spreadsheet to document the number of times studies mentioned a particular antecedent. We used these antecedents to inform the conceptual framework. In developing the conceptual framework for this report, we used Hausknecht and Trevor's (2011) retention model as a starting point and adapted it based on other antecedents we found in literature. After constructing this conceptual framework, we classified antecedents found in our sample of literature in the framework. For example, if a study listed quality of co-workers as an antecedent, we documented the antecedent, the source, and its framework classification (cohesiveness/teamwork).

Appendix E. Considerations and Challenges in Applying Data Science to Air Force Human Resource Problems

One of the most significant developments in human resource management (HRM) during the twenty-first century is the application of tools from data science to HR tasks. The increased use of data science in HRM is attributed to three interrelated developments: (1) the volume, variety, and velocity of data now available;[1] (2) improvements in computational algorithms for extracting meaning from those data;[2] and (3) affordable computing resources to apply algorithms to large amounts of data at speed and scale (Brynjolfsson and Mitchell, 2017). Despite data science being a relatively new concept, consensus has emerged about the potential for data science techniques, including artificial intelligence (AI) and ML, to improve the efficiency and effectiveness of HRM practices (Tonidandel, King, and Cortina, 2018).

Notwithstanding this promise, a commercial organization must deal with several challenges to use AI for HRM (Table E.1).[3] These include (1) developing a digital infrastructure for capturing data and deploying ML systems; (2) defining employee outcomes and associated metrics; (3) adopting ML methods suitable for small and moderately sized data sets; (4) ensuring the ethical and legal use of data sources and model outputs; and (5) tracking employees' experiences with and reactions to algorithmic decision aids.

The Air Force must also address these challenges to use AI for HRM. Some may be less problematic for the Air Force. For example, the size of the total force combined with regular entries to personnel files has resulted in longitudinal data sets comprised of millions of person-month records. Other challenges are equally problematic for the Air Force. For example, outcomes such as career success are hard to define and to objectively measure. Additionally, given the consequential nature of decisions in matters such as promotion and selection for prestigious career development experiences, ML system recommendations must be explainable, defensible, and equitable. Finally, some of these challenges, though equally problematic for the Air Force in general, are less of a concern in the case of a REW system. For example, separation forecasts generated by the ML do not involve individual-level decisions, and so they raise fewer significant concerns about accountability and fairness than a system that makes actual recommendations.

---

[1] Volume refers to the size of a data set, variety refers to the different types of data being combined, and velocity refers to how regularly data are added. See Putka, Beatty, and Reeder, 2018.

[2] Most of these algorithms fall under the heading of ML, a discipline focused on building computer programs that improve their performance automatically through experience. See Jordan and Mitchell, 2015.

[3] Tambe, Cappelli, and Yakubovich, 2019.

Table E.1. Challenges of Introducing Artificial Intelligence to Human Resources Management and Air Force Considerations

Challenge	Description	Air Force Considerations
Digital infrastructure	To apply AI to HRM, data must first be captured, stored, organized, and shared across databases	+ The Air Force captures data about individuals over the complete career life cycle – Data are stored in separate databases and vary in terms of accuracy and completeness
Complexity of HR outcomes	Certain outcomes such as job performance are multidimensional and inherently hard to measure	+ Certain outcomes such as separation are well defined and easily measured – Other outcomes such as suitability for promotion are harder to define and measure
Small data	As compared with other domains where ML has been used, HRM data sets are relatively small	+ The active duty officer inventory contains more than 60,000 officers and 250,000 enlisted personnel – Certain outcomes such as separation occur relatively infrequently – Personnel subgroups of interest defined by multiple features (e.g., race/ethnicity, gender, and career field) may be quite small
Accountability, fairness, and explainability	Given the consequential nature of HRM decisions, the outcomes of ML systems must be explainable, defensible, and equitable	+ The use of AI to predict separations bypasses the need to make individual-level decisions – Analysts and planners must understand the factors influencing projections
Employee reactions	The organization must build employee and manager consensus around the acceptable use of the AI system	+ The use of AI to forecast separations bypasses the need to make individual-level decisions – Analysts and planners must understand the assumptions and limitations of projections

SOURCE: Tambe, Cappelli, and Yakubovich, 2019.

Appendix F. Policy Impact Methodology

Estimated policy impacts are obtained by applying population-level effects to the individual-level retention probabilities estimated by the ML predictions. To do this, we use established methodology from the education literature for evaluating effects sizes of programs with dichotomous outcomes. First, the raw retention effect of a particular (or hypothetical) intervention is converted to a real number using the following formula, recommended by the What Works Clearinghouse *Procedures Handbook* (2017):

$$d = \left[\log\left(\frac{p_i}{1 - p_i}\right) - \log\left(\frac{p_c}{1 - p_c}\right) \right] / 1.65.$$

In the above equation, p_i is the retention rate after intervention, p_c is the retention rate before intervention, and d is the resulting continuous effect size. When applying effect sizes in REWS, we substitute the current average retention rate for p_c and $p_i = p_c + p_\Delta$, where p_Δ is the additive policy effect on retention for separation eligible service members. By rescaling the raw additive retention effect to the continuous effect d, we are appropriately adjusting retention rate effect sizes to take into account the fact that not all effects of equal size on the retention scale should be treated equally. For instance, an increase in retention from 1 percent to 2 percent should be treated as a larger effect than an increase in retention from 50 percent to 51 percent. While both effects represent an additive increase of 1 percent, the first increase represents a doubling in the number of retained servicemembers. The rescaling represented in the above formula attempts reflect this intuition. The scaled effect size d is then added to each scaled individual retention probability before being transformed back to individual-level, post-policy treatment probabilities.

In the Policy Impact page of the REWS application, we supply some sample effects based on published estimates from the research literature for use as informal benchmarks. Figure F.1 reproduces those effects for reference. The user can select a percentage from this table and the REWS application will apply it to the population that is eligible to separate using the procedure described above.

Figure F.1. Suggested Policy Impact Table from the Retention Early Warning System Application

Suggested policy impact inputs.

Research has been done on the impact of particular policies on the retention of military members. The implementation of new policies or the adjustment of existing policies typically requires standalone analyses to understand the impact on retention. However, prior research can be used to suggest impacts.

The estimated retention impacts below should only be used as a guide and are not meant to be precise estimates.

Policy Intervention	Estimated retention impact		Supporting literature and notes
Enlisted			
SRB multiplier increase of 1 unit	0.8% (across all career fields for members in the last year of their first enlistment contract)		Joffrion, Justin L. and Wozny, Nathan, Military Retention Incentives: Evidence from the Air Force Selective Reenlistment Bonus (April 28, 2015). Upjohn Institute Working Paper No. 15-226, https://ssrn.com/abstract=2600046 or http://dx.doi.org/10.2139/ssrn.2600046 Note: Change in the SRB multiplier was not found to affect retention rates of servicemembers outside of those in the last year of their first enlistment contract.
Officers			
$5,000 annual bonus for all YOS	1-5 YOS	0.5%	Mattock, Michael G., Beth J. Asch, James Hosek, Christopher Whaley, and Christina Panis, Toward Improved Management of Officer Retention: A New Capability for Assessing Policy Options. Santa Monica, CA: RAND Corporation, 2014. https://www.rand.org/pubs/research_reports/RR764.html. Note: Estimated changes in retention probabilities are computed using the basic dynamic retention model implemented in the above paper. Importantly, this model is based on an underlying dataset of Army officers. All policy impacts reflect steady-state (i.e. long-term) effects of retention.
	6-10 YOS	2.5%	
	11-15 YOS	1.4%	
	16-20 YOS	0.5%	
	21-25 YOS	1.2%	
	26-30 YOS	0.8%	
$10,000 annual bonus for all YOS	1-5 YOS	1.1%	
	6-10 YOS	4.7%	
	11-15 YOS	2.6%	
	16-20 YOS	0.9%	
	21-25 YOS	2.3%	
	26-30 YOS	1.6%	
$15,000 annual bonus for all YOS	1-5 YOS	1.6%	
	6-10 YOS	6.8%	
	11-15 YOS	3.7%	
	16-20 YOS	1.4%	
	21-25 YOS	3.4%	
	26-30 YOS	2.5%	
$20,000 annual bonus for all YOS	1-5 YOS	2.0%	
	6-10 YOS	8.7%	
	11-15 YOS	4.5%	
	16-20 YOS	1.7%	
	21-25 YOS	4.4%	
	26-30 YOS	3.3%	
Pilots			
$5,000 increase on $25,000 5-year ACP	1-10 YOS	0.0%	Mattock, Michael G., Beth J. Asch, James Hosek, Christopher Whaley, and Christina Panis, Toward Improved Management of Officer Retention: A New Capability for Assessing Policy Options. Santa Monica, CA: RAND Corporation, 2014. https://www.rand.org/pubs/research_reports/RR764.html. Notes: Estimated retention impact refers to retention of pilots only. Changes in retention probabilities are computed using the ACP dynamic retention model implemented in the above paper. All policy impacts reflect steady-state (i.e. long-term) effects of retention.
	11-15 YOS	1.7%	
	16-20 YOS	-0.4%	
	21-25 YOS	-0.6%	
	26-30 YOS	-0.2%	
$10,000 increase on $25,000 5-year ACP	1-10 YOS	0.0%	
	11-15 YOS	2.9%	
	16-20 YOS	-0.8%	
	21-25 YOS	-1.0%	
	26-30 YOS	-0.4%	
$15,000 increase on $25,000 5-year ACP	1-10 YOS	0.0%	
	11-15 YOS	3.8%	
	16-20 YOS	-1.0%	
	21-25 YOS	-1.2%	
	26-30 YOS	-0.5%	
$20,000 increase on $25,000 5-year ACP	1-10 YOS	0.0%	
	11-15 YOS	4.3%	
	16-20 YOS	-1.2%	
	21-25 YOS	-1.4%	
	26-30 YOS	-0.6%	
Increase in commercial airline hiring resulting in a change from 10% to 50% probability of being hired by a commercial airline	1-20 YOS	-6.3%	Mattock, Michael G., James Hosek, Beth J. Asch, and Rita Karam, Retaining U.S. Air Force Pilots When the Civilian Demand for Pilots Is Growing. Santa Monica, CA: RAND Corporation, 2016. https://www.rand.org/pubs/research_reports/RR1455.html. Also available in print form.
	>20 YOS	-15.1%	Notes: Estimated retention impact refers to retention of pilots only. All policy impacts reflect steady-state (i.e. long-term) effects of retention. In the year of the cited study, an increase in the probability of being hired by a commercial airline from 10% to 50% corresponded to an increase in 1,700 to 3,200 airline hires per year.

References

Allaire, J. J., *Deep Learning with R*, Shelter Island, N.Y.: Manning Publications, 2018.

Allen, David G., *Retaining Talent: A Guide to Analyzing and Managing Employee Turnover*, Alexandria, Va.: SHRM Foundation, 2008.

Asch, Beth J., Michael G. Mattock, and James Hosek, *The Blended Retirement System: Retention Effects and Continuation Pay Cost Estimates for the Armed Services*, Santa Monica, Calif.: RAND Corporation, RR-1887-OSD/USCG, 2017. As of September 8, 2020:
https://www.rand.org/pubs/research_reports/RR1887.html

Blinder, Alan S., "Wage Discrimination: Reduced Form and Structural Estimates," *Journal of Human Resources*, Vol. 8, No. 4, Autumn 1973, pp. 436–455.

Breiman, Leo, "Statistical Modeling: The Two Cultures," *Statistical Science*, Vol. 16, No. 3, 2001, pp. 199–231.

Brynjolfsson, Erik, and Tom Mitchell, "What Can Machine Learning Do? Workforce Implications," *Science*, Vol. 358, No. 6370, 2017, pp. 1530–1534.

Chapman, Pete, Julian Clinton, Randy Kerber, Thomas Khabaza, Thomas Teinartz, Colin Shearer, and Rudiger Wirth, *CRISP-DM 1.0: Step-by-Step Data Mining Guide*, The CRISP-DM Consortium, 2000.

Congressional Research Service, *Defense Primer: Personnel Tempo (PERSTEMPO)*, Washington, D.C., 2020. As of November 20, 2020:
https://fas.org/sgp/crs/natsec/IF11007.pdf

Department of the Air Force, *Fiscal Year (FY) 2021 Budget Estimates: Military Personnel Appropriation*, February 2020. As of September 8, 2020:
https://www.saffm.hq.af.mil/Portals/84/documents/FY21/MILPER_/FY21%20Air%20Force%20Military%20Personnel_1.pdf?ver=2020-02-10-091310-847

Hardison, Chaitra M., Michael G. Mattock, and Maria C. Lytell, *Incentive Pay for Remotely Piloted Aircraft Career Fields*, Santa Monica, Calif.: RAND Corporation, MG-1174-AF, 2012. As of September 8, 2020:
https://www.rand.org/pubs/monographs/MG1174.html

Hausknecht, John P., and Charlie O. Trevor, "Collective Turnover at the Group, Unit, and Organizational Levels: Evidence, Issues, and Implications," *Journal of Management*, Vol. 37, No. 1, 2011, pp. 352–388.

Hom, Peter W., David G. Allen, and Rodger W. Griffeth, *Employee Retention and Turnover: Why Employees Stay or Leave*, New York: Routledge, 2020.

Joffrion, Justin, and Nathan Wozny, "Military Retention Incentives: Evidence from the Air Force Selective Reenlistment Bonus," Upjohn Institute Working Paper 15-226, Kalamazoo, Mich.: Upjohn Institute for Employment Research, 2015.

Jordan, M. I., and T. M. Mitchell, "Machine Learning Trends, Perspectives, and Prospects," *Science*, Vol. 349, No. 6245, 2015, pp. 255–260.

Joseph, Damien, Kok-Yee Ng, Christine Koh, and Soon Ang, "Turnover of Information Technology Professionals: A Narrative Review, Meta-Analytic Structural Equation Modeling, and Model Development," *MIS Quarterly*, Vol. 31, No. 3, September 2007, pp. 547–577.

Keller, Kirsten, Kimberly Curry Hall, Miriam Matthews, Leslie Payne, Lisa Saum-Manning, Douglas Yeung, David Schulker, Stefan Zavislan, and Nelson Lim, *Addressing Barriers to Female Officer Retention in the Air Force*, Santa Monica, Calif.: RAND Corporation, RR-2073-AF, 2018. As of April 22, 2021:
https://www.rand.org/pubs/research_reports/RR2073.html

Kiazad, Kohyar, Brooks C. Holtom, Peter W. Hom, and Alexander Newman, "Job Embeddedness: A Multifoci Theoretical Extension," *Journal of Applied Psychology*, Vol. 100, No. 3, May 2015, pp. 641–659.

Kotu, Vijay, and Bala Deshpande, *Data Science*, 2nd ed., Cambridge, Mass.: Elsevier Inc., 2019.

Maertz, C. P., and R. W. Griffeth, "Eight Motivational Forces and Voluntary Turnover: A Theoretical Synthesis with Implications for Research," *Journal of Management*, Vol. 30, No. 5, 2004, pp. 667–683.

Mariscal, Gonzalo, Óscar Marbán, and Covadonga Fernández, "A Survey of Data Mining and Knowledge Discovery Process Models and Methodologies," *The Knowledge Engineering Review*, Vol. 25, No. 2, 2010, pp. 137–166.

Mattock, Michael G., James Hosek, Beth J. Asch, and Rita T. Karam, *Retaining U.S. Air Force Pilots When the Civilian Demand for Pilots Is Growing*, Santa Monica, Calif.: RAND Corporation, RR-1455-AF, 2016. As of June 18, 2021:
https://www.rand.org/pubs/research_reports/RR1455.html

Mattock, Michael G., and Jeremy Arkes, *The Dynamic Retention Model for Air Force Officers: New Estimates and Policy Simulations of the Aviator Continuation Pay Program*, Santa Monica, Calif.: RAND Corporation, TR-470-AF, 2007. As of September 8, 2020:
https://www.rand.org/pubs/technical_reports/TR470.html

Mobley, William H., "Intermediate Linkages in the Relationship Between Job Satisfaction and Employee Turnover," *Journal of Applied Psychology*, Vol. 62, No. 2, 1977, pp. 237–240.

Oaxaca, Ronald, "Male–Female Wage Differentials in Urban Labor Markets," *International Economic Review*, Vol. 14, No. 3, October 1973, pp. 693–709.

Phillips, Jack J., and Lisa Edwards, *Managing Talent Retention: An ROI Approach*, Essential Resources for Training and HR Professionals, San Francisco: Pfeiffer, 2009.

Porter, J. L., and R. M. Steers, "Organizational, Work, and Personal Factors in Employee Turnover and Absenteeism," *Psychological Bulletin*, Vol. 80, 1973, pp. 151–176.

Putka, Dan J., Adam S. Beatty, and Matthew C. Reeder, "Modern Prediction Methods: New Perspectives on a Common Problem," *Organizational Research Methods*, Vol. 21, No. 3, 2018, pp. 689–732.

Salomon, Richard, "AF Officials Launch 2018 Total Force Climate Survey," Air Force Personnel Center Public Affairs, August 2018. As of September 24, 2020: https://www.afpc.af.mil/News/Article-Display/Article/1615946/af-officials-launch-2018 -total-force-climate-survey/

Singh, Niharika, and L. S. Sharma, "Process Models of Employee Turnover During 1975–1995: A Review," *European Academic Research*, Vol. 3, No. 2, 2015, pp. 2494–2518.

Tambe, Prasanna, Peter Cappelli, and Valery Yakubovich, "Artificial Intelligence in Human Resources Management: Challenges and a Path Forward," *California Management Review*, Vol. 61, No. 4, 2019, pp. 15–42.

Tong, Patricia K., Michael G. Mattock, Beth J. Asch, James Hosek, and Felix Knutson, *Modeling Career Enlisted Aviator Retention in the U.S. Air Force*, Santa Monica, Calif.: RAND Corporation, RR-3134-AF, 2020. As of April 23, 2021: https://www.rand.org/pubs/research_reports/RR3134.html

Tonidandel, Scott, Eden B. King, and Jose M. Cortina, "Big Data Methods: Leveraging Modern Data Analytic Techniques to Build Organizational Science," *Organizational Research Methods*, Vol. 21, No. 3, 2018, pp. 525–547.

U.S. Air Force, "Climate Survey Enhancements to Improve Awareness for Commanders," December 13, 2013. As of November 20, 2020: https://www.af.mil/News/Article-Display/Article/467732/climate-survey-enhancements -to-improve-awareness-for-commanders/

———, *Fitness Program*, Air Force Instruction 36-2905, October 21, 2015.

U.S. Air Force Deputy Chief of Staff, Manpower, Personnel, and Services, *Headquarters Mission Directive 1-32*, September 13, 2019.

U.S. Census Bureau, *Current Population Survey Design and Methodology Technical Paper 77*, October 2019. As of September 9, 2020:
https://www2.census.gov/programs-surveys/cps/methodology/CPS-Tech-Paper-77.pdf

———, Methodology of the Current Population Survey, undated. As of May 3, 2021:
https://www.census.gov/programs-surveys/cps/technical-documentation/methodology.html

What Works Clearinghouse, *Procedures Handbook, Version 4.1*, Institute for Education Sciences, National Center for Education Evaluation and Regional Assistance, 2017. As of September 24, 2020:
https://ies.ed.gov/ncee/wwc/Docs/referenceresources/WWC-Procedures-Handbook-v4-1 -508.pdf